Rip-off Tip-offs
Winning the
Auto Repair Game

For Ralph Bennett, good friend and *Reader's Digest* senior staff editor, whose phone call triggered the events that eventually led to the publication of this book.

Rip-off Tip-offs
Winning the
Auto Repair Game

Robert Sikorsky

TAB BOOKS
Blue Ridge Summit, PA

FIRST EDITION
FIRST PRINTING

Copyright © 1990 by TAB BOOKS
Printed in the United States of America

Library of Congress Cataloging in Publication Data

Sikorsky, Robert.
Rip-off tip-offs : winning the auto repair game / by Robert
Sikorsky.
p.   cm.
ISBN 0-8306-9572-9   ISBN 0-8306-3572-6 (pbk.)
1. Automobiles—Maintenance and repair. 2. Consumer education—
United States. I. Title.
TL152.S5232 1990
629.28′72—dc20   89-20683
                                                                              CIP

TAB BOOKS offers software for
sale. For information and a catalog,
please contact TAB Software Department,

Blue Ridge Summit, PA 17294-0850.

Questions regarding the content of this book
should be addressed to:

Reader Inquiry Branch
TAB BOOKS
Blue Ridge Summit, PA 17294-0214

Acquisitions Editor: Kimberly Tabor
Book Editor: Susan L. Rockwell
Production: Katherine Brown

Contents

Foreword

Because it contains so much valuable information, this book can and should be read by a wide audience. It tells car owners the basics of automobile engines and the repair process, so that we can avoid surprises and get a fair deal. It tells honest mechanics (and there are tens of thousands of them) how to earn and maintain customer confidence. It states the laws that every legislator should have to govern auto repair: written estimates, customer-signed repair authorizations, detailed invoices, and used parts returned upon request.

I was also impressed that you spelled out for educators the disturbing but unavoidable fact—if mechanics are not trained, retrained, and kept up to date, they will fail to repair our cars no matter how honest they could be.

This book is really about responsibility—to ourselves and to each other. If our cars are to serve us with the reliability we feel is our right, we must give our cars—and the automotive repair industry—the attention they deserve. *Rip-off Tip-offs: Winning the Auto Repair Game* is a deft and effective treatment of a subject about which virtually no car owner is neutral.

—*Martin B. Dyer*
Chief, California Department of Consumer Affairs,
Bureau of Automotive Repair

How do I choose the right shop to work on my car when something goes wrong, or for check-ups and inspections that should be done periodically? What do I tell the service person or technician so my car will get fixed properly without wasted time and expense?

These questions or doubts bother many people who move into a new community or have a car problem away from home or are not really happy with the shop they went to last for vehicle service or repairs.

As president of AIC, I hear some automotive repair horror stories, but I also hear from many people who are really pleased with the vehicle repairs made by their mechanic or their service shop. Some of the horror stories concern poorly trained technicians, but many are the result of wrong information inadvertently communicated to the technician by the car owner.

Our members want you to be pleased with your vehicle and with your automotive repair shop. In this book, Bob Sikorsky gives you some excellent guidelines that will make it easier for you to choose the right repair shop and to correctly communicate your problem to the shop.

—Robert C. Calderone
President, Automotive Information Council

Rip-off Tip-offs: Winning the Auto Repair Game goes a long way toward educating the motorist on the complexity of finding a fair and comfortable means of achieving proper auto maintenance and repair. Our members applaud your efforts to expose those businesses that are unfair, or employ incompetent help. We also appreciate your information on how the public can find the shops that deserve their business.

—John F. Goodman
Executive Director, Automotive Service Councils

Introduction

Dear Mr. Sikorsky:

How does one go about finding an honest mechanic? We have been ripped off so many times that we now consider it part of the dues we must pay to get the car fixed—$100 repair estimates turn into $500 repair bills. Is there any way to tell a good garage from a bad one?

—An excerpt from a letter to my syndicated column

So you're tired of getting ripped off, tired of shoddy repairs and incompetent mechanics, tired of taking your car back to a shop time and time again trying to get it fixed, tired of paying for parts and services you really don't need—tired, tired, tired. Well you've come to the right place (Fig. 1).

If ever there was a plaintive cry of the American motorist it's "Where can I find an honest, competent mechanic?" Of all the questions I have been asked, that one turns up most frequently. Widows, single men and women, married men and women, old and young, rich or poor—all want to know. Indeed, are there any honest competent mechanics out there?

Well take heart, for there are—lots of them. And they can be found in repair shops most anywhere from a busy street in a big city to a quonset hut on the outskirts of a small town. You might find them in a large franchised shop, a new car dealership's service department, an oil company service station, or in a small or large independent garage. It really doesn't matter. For what you are looking for is a

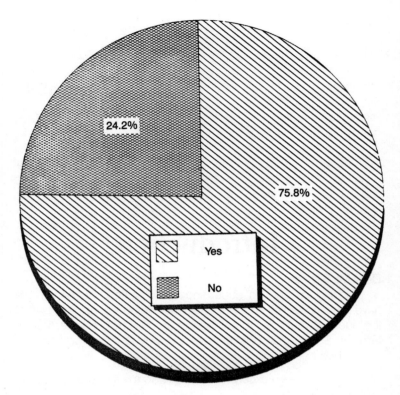

24.2%

75.8%

Yes

No

Fig. 1. Do you feel that the level of distrust of automotive servicing is enough to require correction?

shop and technician that will treat you fairly and your car competently.

Most of us view taking a car in for repairs with trepidation. It's not a pleasant experience. But it doesn't have to be that way. You need to know how to tell a good garage from a bad one and how to spot a cheat or incompetent.

Make no mistake about it, there are dishonest mechanics. They could care less about repairing your car, about giving good service, or about treating you fairly. They are after your money, pure and simple.

And there are many more mechanics, who are not dishonest, but can still wreak havoc with your finances and car. An incompetent mechanic can do just as much harm as one who is out to cheat you from the start. In the long run both cost you money: one intentionally; the other, unintentionally.

There are too many incompetents in this nation's repair shops. Discouragingly, their numbers are holding fast. Too many, for whatever reason, are either unwilling or unable to keep up with current automotive technology. Their uncaring attitude is the bane of every competent repair facility and helps breed more incompetence. Modern technicians must keep abreast of today's rapidly changing and complicated technology in order to treat customers fairly and competently. Mechanics can not bypass this mandate.

Many mechanics are intimidated by computer-controlled cars and automatically assume that any problem has to be either complicated or computer-related. They forget to go back to basics and check the same things they would check in cars without on-board computers. They also forget that electronics and computers only control the engine's functions—the engine itself is relatively unchanged.

Whether you're at home or on the highway, it isn't any fun when your car breaks down. Getting it fixed can be a frustrating, expensive, and sometimes flim-flam affair. We all know the feeling.

Consumers spend a staggering $70 billion dollars each year on automotive upkeep, and the average car owner can expect repairs (not including maintenance, insurance, etc.) to cost $500 or more annually. A typical repair shop charges about $75 per hour for parts and labor. Parts prices, especially for imports, are skyrocketing. If you own an import, that's not news to you. In today's repair climate, you can't pop into a shop, have some work done, and come out with a $15 parts and labor bill. Those days are history.

Even a quick look-see by the technician shouldn't go without its financial rewards. With today's high-tech cars a two-tier system of auto repairs is in effect: the problem must be diagnosed, and the repair effected. That might not sound a whole lot different from what it used to be. The difference now is that diagnostics are more time consuming. For that reason consumers should be prepared to pay for diagnostics as either a separate item (even if the technician didn't fix the problem), or added to the final repair bill (Fig. 2).

We are still in the throes of an automotive computer and electronics revolution. Computer controls, although common in almost every new car, are still novel enough that some mechanics view them as a passing fancy. They aren't.

As we wind our way into the '90s, the technician who goes with the flow and is not intimidated by new technology, is finding that the actual repair of most computer- and electronic-controlled cars is, for the most part, simpler than in the old days (Fig. 3). The on-board computers themselves are lending a helping hand because many are

Customer billing—

- Customers must pay for diagnostic time, if the customer's expectations are to be met.
- The customer expects their problem to be corrected with one visit!
- Shops trying to develop a good reputation must meet the customer's expectation!
- Customers will pay for excellence!

Fig. 2. Make sure you keep these points in mind.

capable of diagnosing their own problems (marvel of marvels!) and pointing the knowledgeable technician in the right repair direction. This book will guide you to these up-to-date competent technicians and repair shops where fair prices and thorough work are the norm.

Today's technology—

- Diagnosis is more complex than yesterday.

- Repair is less complex than yesterday.

- Diagnosis is more important than ever before!

Fig. 3. Modern problems still must be diagnosed and repaired.

Highway Robbery:
The Scandal of Auto Repair

In the fall of 1986, *Reader's Digest* asked me to conduct a national survey. I visited over 225 repair facilities of all kinds to find if Americans are getting honest and competent automobile repair. My report appeared in the May 1987 issue and stirred up more interest than any *Reader's Digest* article in recent years (Fig. 1-1).

More than 300 newspapers commented on the article, from front page coverage in *USA Today* to *The Washington Post*. It sparked heated controversy in the automotive trade press and was featured on scores of television and radio programs, from Paul Harvey to "Hour Magazine," and Betty Furness and Regis Philbin to CNN's "Sonja in LA."

Trade publications still expound upon the impact of "Highway Robbery." It was that article, and the subsequent furor and interest it created, that convinced me a book of this type was necessary. An official of CARS, the Congress of Automotive Repair and Service, was indeed on the mark when he said, "This single article will be reverberating throughout our business for years to come." The article is reprinted here in its entirety.

Are Americans getting a square deal for the $65 billion they spend each year to maintain their cars? To find out, *Reader's Digest* bought a typical used car—a 1984 Oldsmobile Cutlass Ciera sedan (one of the biggest-selling U.S. cars that year) with 20,000 miles on the odometer.

Under the supervision of a consulting mechanic and project editor Ralph Bennett, an Oldsmobile dealer made the car like new:

Fig. 1-1. USA Today headlined the Reader's Digest *article.*

engine tuned, transmission serviced, new spark plugs, brakes, shock absorbers, struts, fan belts, and hoses. Every vital component was thoroughly checked and, if there was any doubt, replaced.

Then we put our blue-gray Olds on the road. Behind the wheel: nationally syndicated automotive columnist Robert Sikorsky, author of the bestseller *Drive It Forever* and veteran of hundreds of road tests. Bob's assignment: travel the country, pick repair garages at random, and see how they treat a customer in need.* Bob pulled the same single spark-plug wire loose from the V-6 engine just before each stop, thus making the motor run roughly.

A loose wire is something that even a novice mechanic should notice. Reattaching it to the plug was all that was necessary to put our car in perfect running condition. But many mechanics either didn't spot the problem or fraudulently corrected it by selling or recommending a wide array of parts, oils, and solvents.

What Bob Sikorsky discovered after stops at 225 garages should be a warning to every car owner. Here is Bob's account of his 10,000 mile safari through America's auto-repair jungle.

My engine was faltering as I pulled up at a large independent garage in Old Saybrook, Connecticut, one morning last September. I told the mechanic my car "wasn't running right."

As he opened the hood, I heard the sharp cracking sound of a loose plug wire "shorting out" against the engine block. Ignoring that symptom, the mechanic slowly removed the oil-filler cap. With a grave look, he stuck a long screwdriver into the opening and placed an ear against the wooden handle. Like a doctor with a stethoscope, he listened to the engine.

"You got a bad rocker," he said. Beckoning me inside the garage, he staged an impressive show-and-tell, swiveling the rocker

---

*Our survey was not intended to be a statistical exercise, but rather was an effort to show what an average motorist in need of car repair might encounter.

arms (they open the engine valves) on a rocker shaft he had picked off the floor.

He phoned about replacement parts, meanwhile congratulating me for coming to his garage. "You're going to save about half over what a dealer would charge."

The repair would take three hours and cost $125 to $175. But, he warned, there might be other problems once he "got inside" the engine. I told him I'd think it over. I drove away, pulled off the road, and pushed the wire back onto the spark plug, restoring the car to smooth running condition.

Fair Game. That wire, about the length and thickness of a garter snake, would bite time and time again as I sought repairs at gas stations, dealerships, independent garages, and chain automotive outlets in 33 states. My experience made me acutely aware why so many Americans complain about their treatment in the nation's 300,000 auto-repair shops.

■ Only 28 percent of my stops resulted in a correct diagnosis and repair. Three out of four times, I was either denied service, had to wait for hours (or days), or was victimized by dishonesty, incompetence, or both.

■ When a mechanic did work on the car, I got a satisfactory repair only 44 percent of the time.

■ In the other 56 percent, mechanics performed unnecessary work, sold unnecessary parts, or charged for repairs not done. Worse, some of their work created new engine problems.

Make no mistake, I met a lot of good, honest mechanics, but their reputation is unfairly stained by a large number of mechanics who either don't know what they are doing or treat motorists as fair game or fools.

My loose wire provoked a slew of remedies, including spark-plug cleaning, major and minor tune-ups, valve adjustment, correction of fuel starvation, carburetor adjustment, and even transmission rebuilding.

Among parts recommended were fuel filters, gasoline additives, catalytic converters, air pumps, engine-control modules, distributor caps and rotors, and valve lifters. In all, more than 100 useless remedies were prescribed, priced from $2 to more than $500.

One blitz of rip-offs began in Jacksonville, Florida. At five consecutive shops, cures included a distributor cap ($30), a set of plug wires ($70), a set of spark plugs ($30), a single spark plug ($8.93), and the end of the plug wire ($17.27).

Deciding it was time to get out of Jacksonville, I headed north. In Brunswick, Georgia, a mechanic spotted the loose wire but attached it to a new plug ($17.36), replacing the one installed in Jacksonville just 65 miles earlier! Next stop-Savannah, where two successive shops recommended tune-ups for $184 (including new plug wires) and $101 (with new plug wires "highly recommended" at extra cost).

Chain Reaction. Big-city shops were much more likely to go after my wallet than small-town and rural garages were. The presence of nationally certified mechanics did not guarantee good service. In fact, I got gypped in 50 percent of the shops boasting nationally certified technicians. I received excellent treatment in some pretty crude garages, and got taken to the cleaners in some fancy shops complete with coffee, courtesy, and the latest technology.

I found, too, that car owners are often victims of shoddy repairs that cause other problems. When a Kansas City, Missouri, mechanic replaced (unnecessarily) a gas filter, he forgot to reinstall the spring that holds the filter in place. I limped into a garage in Salina, Kansas, where a mechanic found the spring lying on the manifold and also discovered that my carburetor air-cleaner gasket had not been reinstalled.

Occasionally there were breathtaking instances of outright fraud. One of these began early one morning in Tucson, Arizona.

As I pumped gas at a service station beside Interstate 10, a wiry fellow in work clothes sauntered out and hunkered down on the other side of the car. That's nice, I thought. He's checking my tire pressure.

"I see you've got new shocks," he said. "Good, but your coil springs are bent." Coil springs do wear out, and can bend under extremely rare conditions, but this was definitely not the case with our low-mileage car. The attendant said he just happened to have a set that he could install for $125.

I drove away without the new coil springs, but I couldn't help thinking about hapless motorists who might have been frightened into having them installed.

Fishing for Profits. Another memorable encounter took place in San Antonio when I pulled into a transmission-repair shop. The owner test-drove the Olds with me in the passenger seat. As we climbed a hill, the car seemed to be straining. I looked down and noted that he had one foot on the gas and the other on the brake.

"Boy, it ain't got no power at all in second gear," he said. "It's real obvious the clutches are burnt." His solution: rebuild the transmission for $395 to $495, "depending on if I can save the torque converter."

One device the motorist with engine trouble is almost certain to run into is the *scope*, an electronic engine analyzer. In honest, competent hands, the concept is great; you let the high-tech detective with its switches, dials, and oscilloscopes sort out the problem. Trouble is, these devices vary in accuracy, and their operators vary widely in ability to interpret them.

At a national retailer's auto-care center in Biloxi, Mississippi, two mechanics plugged a hand-held computer into an outlet under my dash. The computer was supposed to interface with the car's diagnostic system and print out the potential source of the problem. The mechanics worked for an hour, never bothering to look for a loose wire.

Finally they produced a printout indicating, they said, that I needed a new distributor cap and rotor. The loud snapping sound (of the shorting plug wire) was, they claimed, coming from the fuel-adjustment solenoid on the carburetor. I paid the scope charge of $16.93, returned to the car, lifted the loose plug wire, and asked one of the mechanics if this might be the problem. Shrugging, he turned and walked away.

The good mechanics I met used the scope intelligently, usually to quickly confirm that my loose plug wire was the only problem. But often the scope was nothing more than a fishing rod to pull in profits on unnecessary repairs.

In Hays, Kansas, at another large chain-store auto center, two technicians fiddled with the car for an hour trying a new distributor cap and rotor, apparently not noticing the loose wire inches away. They hooked the car to an engine analyzer, but still couldn't spot the real problem. They said the trouble was a bad leak in the intake manifold. They were clearly groping, but at least in this case it cost me only $5.73.

It seemed apparent from many encounters that some mechanics are intimidated by the new high-tech cars. They assume that any problems with them must be exotic, and they forget to go back to trade-school basics, such as visually checking for loose wires and hoses. The scope is assumed to be the high-tech answer, but in inept hands, these machines often hinder rather than help.

A New Cure-All. At a service station near the Pennsylvania Turnpike in Carlisle, Pennsylvania, three employees gathered to look under the hood of my car. They never started the engine, but immediately decided to replace the fuel filter. One of them also said the distributor cap and rotor might be the problem. I refused the $90 estimate for the cap and rotor. But this encounter—in which, I must emphasize, the mechanics never started the engine—still cost me $25.44.

As I progressed on my trip, I found that fuel filters have become the modern cure-all for engine troubles. Filters are a critical component of modern fuel systems, but barring unusual circumstances (a tank of bad gas), they should last 15,000 miles or more.

I stopped at a station in Baker, California. Without pausing to listen to my faltering engine, the mechanic said, "I know what your problem is." He began replacing a filter installed a few days earlier in Laramie, Wyoming, so I asked how the "old" one looked. He blew through it before observing sagely. "It's pretty well clogged." I left the station $11 lighter, my engine still stumbling, and the plug wire still dangling.

At a gas station in Lordsburg, New Mexico, two mechanics mused on any number of ills for my poorly running engine. They quickly began changing—you guessed it—the fuel filter. A silver Ford van lurched to a stop nearby. A woman got out and announced, "My truck's broke." One mechanic threw open the hood. "Sounds like a fuel filter to me." He was busily installing one as I refused a $200 estimate for replacing my air pump and distributor cap.

Small Rip-Offs. As I headed out of Lordsburg, I recalled something I had heard a man say in a repair shop waiting room in Massachusetts: Oh, I know I'll probably get taken. I just hope it isn't for too much." Sad to say, many people seem prepared to pay for hidden incompetence or fraud tax on repairs.

But millions of others don't even dream they are being victimized. Whether it's a fuel filter, oil additive, or phantom-plug cleaning, these $20 or $30 bites can add up. For an unscrupulous garage, running enough of these small rip-offs through the cash register is a lot safer than going for a huge swindle that might bring local authorities onto the scene.

I found such scams especially prevalent at stations along interstates, where the chance of a traveler coming back to complain is almost nil. The easiest is the phony repair. In Beaumont, Texas, a garage owner said with good humor, "Eighteen dollars and seventy-five cents is all I can do to you" for replacing a plug wire. But he had merely reattached the one I had loosened.

In Tucson, my wife took the car, with the plug wire loose, to the auto center of a national retailer she has grown to trust. Somebody reconnected the wire. But she was charged $29.99 for a "carburetor adjustment" and a timing check. The carburetor on our 1984 Olds was factory-sealed, and should not be adjusted.

Spark-plug Sabotage. "Here's your problem," the smiling mechanic in a Salt Lake City garage told me. He held up a spark-plug wire. It had a "bad cut," he said, that was causing our engine to misfire.

Indeed, the wire was cut—freshly cut. There was a neat half-inch incision clear around the insulation, which had not been there when I pulled the wire from the plug less than a half-hour before. The mechanic had replaced the wire with a new blue one, and the car ran fine. Bill: $24.75.

At a garage an hour northeast of Las Vegas a few days later, I walked to the back of the car while the mechanic peered under the hood, and I could see his elbow working furiously as he tugged and twisted something. "I found your problem," he announced triumphantly.

He held aloft the same blue wire that had been replaced in Salt Lake City. But the end that fits over the spark plug had been broken off. (Try breaking the end off a plug wire sometime: you really have to work at it.) He repaired the wire for $15.30.

By the end of my trip, I found it difficult to account for the range of prices I encountered. I found a set of plug wires with a five-year guarantee in an auto store for $15.99. A set at an Olds dealer in Tucson cost $53.76. Estimates for a set plus installation ranged from just under $50 in Omaha to $82.60 in Wheeling, West Virginia.

MECHANICS WHO FIND A WAY TO HELP

During my two months on the road, experiences with good, honest garages and mechanics were beacons of reassurance. Project editor Ralph Bennett and I, for example, were driving east on Interstate 10 near Las Cruces, New Mexico, when our "check engine" light came on.

We limped off an exit into Las Cruces, smiling at each other over the irony of it all. Now we had *real* car trouble.

Ralph nursed the car into the parking lot of Wallace Chevrolet-Oldsmobile-Cadillac. By this time the car was missing so badly it was shaking all over. This was the worst time to arrive at a garage—late Friday afternoon. Service adviser, Milt Scott, was juggling paper work and customers as we explained our problem. We did not tell him who we were. Though he was already "ten cars behind," he told us to pull the car into the garage.

Marshall Lincoln, the service manager, personally took charge of the trouble-shooting. We later learned he is one of the top-rated General Motors technicians. But, the problem was difficult to track down. He and Scott stayed several hours after closing, examining the Olds.

Early the next morning (the shop is officially closed on Saturdays), Lincoln finally located the problem by tearing down the carburetor. A piece of Teflon tape, detritus from a previous needless fuel-filter installation, had lodged in one of the carburetor passages.

The unfailing courtesy, professionalism, and the dogged determination to solve the problem showed by the people at Wallace were outstanding. And as Milt Scott pointed out later, *our* attitude helped. "You didn't come into the place demanding this or that. You showed an understanding of our problems on a busy Friday afternoon. Customer attitude means a lot too."

The people at Wallace displayed the one typical characteristic of all the good places we ran across: even if they were extremely busy, they found a way to at least try and help.

In Highland, Indiana, at PTL Tire and Auto, mechanic Ed Nelson quickly spotted the problem: "Sounds like a plug wire arcing." He fixed it, and when he found I was only traveling through, gave the engine a quick but thorough check-over. Charge? Ed and the manager said forget it; they knew what it's like to be on the road.

Indeed, in every case where I got good treatment, the mechanic spotted the loose wire within minutes and sometimes seconds, and half of them refused any money for finding and correcting the problem. Among these were Griffith Shell in Mobile, Alabama; Whisler Chevrolet in Rock Springs, Wyoming; William Mitchell Olds-Cadillac in Pascagoula, Mississippi; Erf's Garage in Glendale, California; and Wade's Country Repair, near Williamsburg, Iowa.

The pleasant experiences I did have confirm that courtesy and competence are still good business.

Your Best Safeguards. My experiences with garages, which strongly suggest you have a less than 50-50 chance of getting fair, competent repair on your first try, make simple precautions all the more imperative. Automotive experts have made these points again and again, but car owners still ignore them.

The "prevent" defense. The most important weapon you have is knowledge of your car. Read the owner's manual. Understand the basics. Does your car have a carburetor or fuel injection? Four cylinders or six? Have a mechanic point out the basic under-hood geography so you can check your oil and coolant levels and spot a loose wire or hose. Follow a regular maintenance plan (oil changes and such) to prevent trouble. A Department of Transportation study shows that the three leading causes of on-the-road breakdowns are bad tires, running out of gas, and cooling-system problems. All three could largely be avoided by a check-before-you-drive inspection.

When you find an honest, competent garage, patronize it regularly. The few dollars you might think you're saving with a bargain oil-change here, a cut-rate tune-up there, cannot compare with work done at a garage that knows your car and wants to keep you as a customer. If you have a problem, it's better to work it out with a service manager or mechanic you know, rather than someone who figures he'll never see you again. If you haven't found a good place, get a recommendation from friends, especially those who keep their cars in good shape.

If you run into trouble away from home and have time, ask the local Better Business Bureau if there are complaints against the garage you have selected. At the garage:

Be specific in describing your car's symptoms. Try to speak directly to the mechanic. If possible, accompany him on a test drive. If major work is recommended, insist on getting a diagnosis elsewhere. At the second garage, describe the trouble without giving the previous shop's diagnosis. If the diagnoses match, chances are the recommendation is correct.

Insist on a detailed written estimate and the assurance that no extra work will be done without your permission. This is required by law in some states. Moreover, be wary of scare tactics ("Lady, I wouldn't drive this car another mile"). Also be wary of someone who tries to rush you into a major repair, insisting he can do it "right away." If possible, pay with a credit card. This will let you stop payment until a dispute is settled.

When precautions fail: complain. This is the most important rule. Do not accept even small rip-offs. Often you will find that what seems to have been fraud was a mistake or misunderstanding that can be straightened out agreeably. But where incompetence or dishonesty is obvious, complain *effectively*. Inform the shop:

■ You are notifying authorities, such as the consumer-fraud unit of the local or state government.
■ You are notifying the Better Business Bureau. The BBB records complaints and informs the garages in question.
■ You are notifying any national organization connected with the shop, such as the American Automobile Association or a major oil, tire, or automotive-products company. These organizations are interested in improving service and will investigate complaints involving their good name.

Marilyn Berton, a special agent of the Arizona attorney general's office, says, "Complaints are our main source of leads in auto-fraud cases. Write a letter or phone us, even if you haven't actually been ripped-off but an attempt has been made."

A series of complaints caused the state of Michigan to launch "Operation Shifty" last year. Investigators were able to close down several dishonest transmission-repair shops in the Detroit area and win money back for victims. A reader of my column, defrauded by a garage, stopped payment on her check, had her attorney tell the shop why, and filed complaints with the BBB and the state attorney general. The shop later closed down.

Low-level Infection. My months on the road show that despite the large number of good, honest mechanics, auto repair still involves a disturbing amount of flimflam. This problem, we believe, is much more serious than the increasing complexity of today's cars, which is creating a gap between the latest technology and the average mechanic's know-how. That can be at least partially overcome with training and information. Chiseling cannot.

Despite the money Americans put into their cars, most people remain woefully ignorant of their car's basics. Unscrupulous garages prey on that ignorance. When you add to this a "what's the use?" attitude among car owners, it's no wonder that—according to one government estimate—32 cents of every dollar that we spend on car repair goes for unneeded work and parts.

There is simply no reason why auto-repair fraud should continue to be tolerated like some low-level infection we motorists can't shake. And the first people who would like to see a cure—through heightened motorist awareness and a willingness to confront the rip-off artists—are the tens of thousands of honest mechanics and garage owners whose reputations suffer unfairly.

2

Getting Recommendations

All of the surveys you have ever read, all of the newspaper horror stories about bad service, and all of your personal experience about inadequate repair delivery are true.

—David A. Evans,
"Is Service For You?" *Automotive Marketing*,
February 1988

REPUTATION: A PRELUDE TO RECOMMENDATION

One of the easiest and best ways to find a good repair shop is one of the most obvious: by recommendation. We do it with doctors, lawyers, and dentists. We ask a friend, relative, neighbor, work associate, or acquaintance who they go to and if they are happy with the service, work, and price. Use the same technique to find a mechanic. In these days of rapidly changing high-technology vehicles, a repair technician is just as important to our welfare as are the above three. Just go a day or two without your car, and you will notice how dependent you are upon it.

There are two kinds of recommendations—for and against—and either can help you find a good mechanic. If someone recommends a shop because they are satisfied with the service they get there, it's one that you should place high on your list. On the other hand, if they recommend you don't go to a particular shop, that advice can save you a lot of frustration and money.

Recommendation then, should be first and foremost on your list of ways to find a good shop. But, I hear you say, you've just moved into town, or this city is so big that you don't know anyone well enough to ask. You can still ask your landlord, the guy at the filling station where you buy your gas, or your boss at work. Although you don't know these people very well, they can still offer a starting point. It's highly unlikely anyone, even a stranger, would purposely recommend a bad shop. I doubt if you will hear "Go to Joe's Garage, I got ripped off there just last week." After weighing the merits of the recommended shop by using the methods in this book, you can make the final decision.

If you're traveling, recommendations from locals—police officers, motel clerks, waitresses, auto-parts store personnel—can prove helpful. During my nationwide trip, I stopped to have a cup of coffee at a roadside cafe and asked the waitress if she knew of a good repair facility. She did, and gave me the name of a shop nearby, at the same time warning me about another one down the road where she said she was ripped-off.

I went to the shop she recommended and sure enough got honest and competent service. To satisfy my curiosity, I also tried the shop she advised against, and just like she had warned, got gypped with service and parts I didn't need.

If the party recommending a shop knows someone working there, be a name dropper. It helps break the ice, and it's always nice to be able to say "Joe Doakes recommended your shop to me, Jack."

A READER RECOMMENDED MECHANIC'S LIST

Prior to becoming nationally syndicated I wrote automotive columns for the *Arizona Daily Star* in Tucson. One column dealt with the trouble people have finding a good mechanic, and after it appeared, a number of readers wrote to say they were lucky because they had a good shop. Most were willing to share the shop names with other readers.

I solicited all readers to write and give me the names of repair shops they were happy with, shops they would feel comfortable recommending to other readers. I received the names of about 40 different shops, a number of them recommended by more than one reader.

I then made a list of these garages, highlighting the ones that had been recommended more than once and called it my *Reader Recommended Mechanics List*. I offered it free-of-charge to anyone who sent me a self-addressed stamped envelope. The newspaper was bowled over with mail. Nearly 4,500 people wrote to get that list of recommended mechanics! It was the largest outpouring of mail the *Star* has ever received!

I was amazed. Was the problem that bad? Were people that hungry to find a good mechanic? My experiences over the next few years, underscored by the *Reader's Digest* findings, convinced me they were—and still are.

But the best part was yet to come. Out of the thousands of readers that requested the list, not one ever expressed dissatisfaction with any of the recommended repair shops. If anything ever pointed out the value of a good recommendation, that list did. Many newcomers later wrote to thank me for guiding them to a good shop, in what to them was a strange town.

"RECOMMENDED" READING: THE PHONE BOOK YELLOW AND WHITE PAGES

If you can't get a recommendation then check the phone book yellow pages. "Let your fingers do the walking" under the Automobile Repairing and Service heading. Under this section you will see how many and what kinds of garages are in your immediate area.

After you have singled out a few shops—in large cities there will be plenty of shops so you can choose those closest to your home— look in the white pages for the Better Business Bureau and consumer protection agencies of the local government.

Consumer protection agencies are sometimes a branch of the city attorney general's office or a local office of the state attorney general. Other city, county, and state offices have separate consumer protection divisions. Every state and its larger cities has consumer protection agencies.

A few minutes spent on calls to these agencies are well worth your time. Ask them for a verbal report, or, if you are not in a hurry, a written one, on the shop you are considering. If you find that there are unresolved complaints on record against the shop, or if legal action has been taken or is pending, cross it off your list. Why invite trouble?

An excellent source for names and addresses of these consumer protection offices is the *Consumer's Resource Handbook*, a United States government publication. It's free, and I highly recommend it. (See Chapter 11 for ordering information.)

You can also go to or call an automotive parts store and ask if they know of a good shop or have an opinion about one you are considering. These people are in touch with many technicians and can be helpful if you are in a strange town. While on the road in the midwest, I heard a number of radio commercials advertising with that approach. "When you need a professional mechanic, we can tell you about some of the best. Just ask," so went a Big A Auto Parts commercial on WHB in Kansas City, and later on KLOE in western Kansas. So take their—and my—advice and ask.

There are differences between finding a shop at home and on the road. At home, you have the luxury of time—if an emergency repair isn't needed—to compare shops. On the road, time is compressed, and comparison shopping isn't practical. If a car has serious trouble and can't be moved, the problem is compounded. But trouble on the road shouldn't be reason for despair. You can still find the best service possible under the circumstances.

Again start with recommendations. Locals, as shown in my waitress example, can be valuable sources. If you are in or near a large city, the BBB and local consumer protection agencies can still provide information on the shop your fate has drawn.

Here's another tip you might want to consider when traveling. Check the phone book for the church you belong to and call its pastor, priest, or rabbi. Ask him if he knows of a good repair shop. Be certain to tell the shop owner that the Reverend Jones or Mr. Parishioner recommended his shop. This isn't as harebrained as it might sound for one shop owner tells me that churches send a lot of customers his way because they know he gives honest service.

The nice thing about going to a recommended shop is that someone else has already culled out some of the questionable shops you might otherwise stumble across. The person recommending a shop probably had a number of bad experiences before settling on the shop he or she uses. That saves you time, effort, money, and a lot of frustration.

A number of technicians I've talked to tell me that they don't take transient trade because people on the road feel that because they are traveling they should be given immediate service. Their regular customers come first. Keep that in mind when you need on-the-road repairs. Courtesy, consideration, and patience will go a long way in helping you get your car repaired—perhaps even at a shop that normally doesn't take on-the-road business.

If you're looking for a repair shop on Saturday afternoon or Sunday—no matter where you are—it won't take long to realize it is almost impossible to find shops that stay open on the weekends.

Years ago my wife and I drove from Arizona to Panama and

Fig. 2-1. "Otto Mechanic" cartoon. "Otto Mechanic"© 1988 BY JAY PIERSANTI. *OLD CARS WEEKLY*.

back. While in Costa Rica the U-joint on our car began to chirp. We stopped in San Jose because we didn't want to chance the then dreaded stretch of road over the Cerro Del Muerto (Mountain of Death) that lay just to the south.

The only shop we could find was jammed. After describing our situation to the mechanic, he moved a number of cars out of the way, verbalizing our plight to his waiting customers. Everyone, the mechanics and the customers, rallied to our support. The customers seemed more than happy to give up their prime spots, and the mechanic more than willing to drop everything to get us back on the road again. It was an exhilarating experience that left us with a warm feeling for Costa Rica and its people, especially its mechanics.

Many of the people working in service stations, tire shops, quick lubes, and other specialty shops aren't mechanics. You're just asking for trouble if you insist that an unqualified party works on your car.

When on the road, it's rare to pull off an interstate intersection and find a full-service repair shop. Almost always you have to rely on service station personnel. But many of them aren't qualified. Would you trust someone making $3.50 an hour pumping gas with your $20,000 machine? The car owner's first responsibility is to himself and you must determine, before having a car worked on, that the mechanics are really mechanics and not just part-time weekend help.

3

Checking Out a
Prospective Repair Shop

Taking your car to a mechanic can be a lot like going to the dentist:
Chances are it will be painful, it will cost more than you originally
thought, and you'll probably be numb when you leave.

—What you probably thought before reading this book

Auto repair shops aren't created equal. Each can't do every type of
repair. You shouldn't take your car to the corner service station to
have your digital dash fixed nor should you expect a quick lube to
fathom the mysteries of an engine malfunction. Unfortunately many
of us do just that. Choosing a repair shop involves more than just
pulling into the first oil-splattered driveway.

The OTEC Division of SPX Corporation reports that in a recent
survey, 3,000 consumers were queried about their automotive service experiences. They were asked what service is the most difficult
to find, what they thought was the cause of any problem or problems
they had with a repair and how repair quality can be improved. Their
answers are reflected in Figs. 3-1, 3-2, and 3-3.

Repair shops are as different as the people that own them. And
just like their owners they come in all sizes, shapes, ages, states of
repair (sorry!), and cleanliness and have different amounts and kinds
of equipment, mechanics, and technicians. Although it would be nice
to standardize repair shops, that's far from being reality. Let's see
what an ideal or preferred shop looks like, keeping in mind that all of
the attributes of an ideal shop might be hard to find in any one shop in

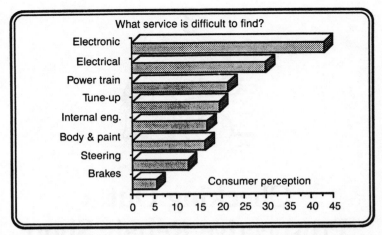

Fig. 3-1. Unfortunately, customers have a hard time finding service for electronic repair.

the real world. But the more pluses you find, the better your chances of getting a competent repair.

AT THE SHOP

Don't be afraid to look the shop over. After all, it's you and your car that will be spending both time and money there. Talk to the manager, the technicians, and the owner. What feeling comes across to

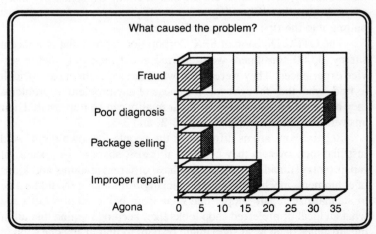

Fig. 3-2. Many times, the diagnosis not only skips over the problem but causes other ones as well.

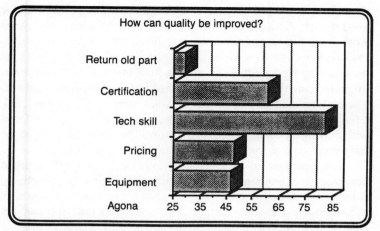

Fig. 3-3. *Today, we are in need of skilled technicians to service our hi-tech cars.*

you? Are they courteous? Do they seem genuinely interested in your problem or are they more preoccupied with talking to a friend? If their attitude is one of "we're too busy to take time to talk to you" or if they don't care that you are taking time to look them over, pick another shop.

A flier, entitled "Why Customers Quit," that I came across at a new car dealership impressed me with its forceful message. It gives customers' reasons, with percentages, for leaving a repair shop:

1%	Die
3%	Move away
5%	Develop other friendships
9%	Leave for competitive reasons
14%	Develop product dissatisfaction
68%	Quit because of an employee's indifferent attitude toward customers

Repair shop owners and employees should make careful note of those numbers and pay attention to their customers.

Talk to the shop's customers. Are they pleased with the service and prices charged? Do they believe that the shop is a good one? Are they regulars? Would they bring their car back again? A good shop won't mind—in fact, it will probably encourage—these inquiries. A questionable one might object.

If a shop is busy, that could indicate that good work is being done there. A shop with little or no business might be that way for good reason. A bustling shop is probably busy because it does good work at fair prices, and the customers trust the employees. It's highly unlikely that customers would keep returning to the same shop if they were getting ripped-off. A shop with little or no activity; however, might indicate that car owners have had bad past experiences there. There's an old adage that says if you want something done right, ask a busy person. Although there is no guarantee, if you are ever faced with making a choice, chances are you will be better off going to the busy shop—just as you would be going to a busy person.

The appearance of the customer waiting area might offer clues to how the whole business is run. A clean neat waiting room probably is indicative of a clean neat shop. It's always nice to find a shop with a comfortable customer lounge. But as I found out, you can get ripped-off while reading a magazine and sipping courtesy coffee in an air-conditioned waiting room as well as while waiting in a dirty, stuffy, and cramped one. It's nice to be comfortable, but it isn't a requirement nor is it a sure-fire signal that a shop does good, honest work. Appearance alone should not be the sole barometer of a shop.

A shop with a library of reference material is more likely to fix your car faster and better than one without. A good reference center is invaluable to a technician. Just as a doctor occasionally goes to his books to bone up, so too must a technician. An up-to-date library also shows that the shop is interested in keeping abreast of current technology—and with today's cars, keeping current is a must.

If the rates for repairs aren't posted, ask. Some shops charge a flat hourly rate published in one of the standard flat rate manuals. Others pay their mechanics on a commission basis (a percentage of the total job price) while still others charge by piece work. An engine diagnostic check might cost a flat rate of $35, regardless of how long it takes. Replacing a clutch might be rated in the hourly flat rate manual as a 5-hour job. The shop then multiplies that time by their hourly rate, adds the cost of parts, and that becomes your bill. Be certain you understand how you will be charged and for what.

A WELL-EQUIPPED SHOP IS A BETTER SHOP

If you own a new car with a computer-controlled engine, determine if the shop is equipped to handle computer servicing and electronic-control repair. As we can see from Fig. 3-1, consumers are already having trouble locating effective electronic and electrical service for their vehicles. And it isn't going to get any easier to find.

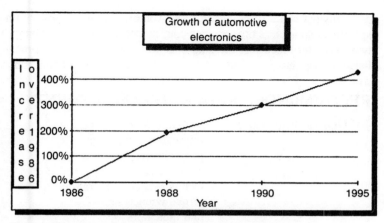

Fig. 3-4. Electronic growth in the auto industry is skyrocketing.

Compared to 1986, 1995 is projected to show a 400 percent increase in growth of automotive electronics.

To efficiently work on today's high-tech cars, sophisticated diagnostic equipment is required (See chapter 4). A well-equipped modern shop should service computer-controlled cars. Their modern equipment is a statement that the owner is keeping up with current technology and is interested in servicing your new car and not just precomputer models.

A full service shop should have complete sets of hand tools for each technician. Also desirable is other equipment such as an alignment pit, a lube and oil change area, hydraulic lifts, and more. Before a repair facility is granted approval from the American Automobile Association (AAA) as an "AAA Approved Repair Shop," it must provide service in engine tune-up, minor engine repair, brakes, electrical systems, and either tires, steering and suspension, or heating and air conditioning areas. In addition, the facility can also provide major engine repairs, automatic transmission, manual transmission, rear axle repairs, and a diagnostic lane.

This book was written to give you every possible edge in tracking down a good repair shop. Although most readers won't go through the bother—in fact, you will need a lot of time and mechanical knowledge to fully appraise all of a shop's equipment—if you really want to be thorough, the AAA's list of equipment requirements is an excellent guide. These are the tools and equipment AAA requires its approved facilities to have. It might not be a bad idea for your shop to have as many as possible.

This list can also be handy when you are seeking a repair in a specific area, such as tires, suspension, or steering. If your investigation has determined that the shop has all or most of the equipment listed in that category, it most likely will be able to do a better job.

RECOMMENDED REPAIR SHOP EQUIPMENT

General Equipment:
vehicle lifts or hoists
lubrication equipment
parts cleaner
safety stands
technical service literature
torque wrench set
dial indicators
gas welding equipment
jacks

Engine Tune-up:
oscilloscope
voltmeter, ammeter, ohmmeter
dwellmeter, tachometer
timing light
vacuum gauge
compression tester
propane gas bottle (carburetor lean-drop check)

Minor Engine Repair:
hand held tools only

Brakes:
brake drum and disc lathe
pressure brake bleeder
dial indicators
brake drum micrometer

Electrical:
voltmeter (0-16 volts)
ohmmeter, ammeter
battery-load tester
battery charger
alternator, regulator, starting circuit tester
belt tension gauge

Tires, Steering, Suspension:	alignment rack
	wheel balancer
	tire and wheel run-out indicator
	coil-spring compressor
	tire changer

Heating and Air Conditioning:	radiator and cap-pressure tester
	AC recharging station
	AC leak detector
	vacuum pump
	manifold gauge set

Major Engine Repair:	engine repair stand
	engine floor crane
	micrometers
	valve refacer, valve-seat cutter
	torque wrench set
	cylinder honer/deglazer
	dial indicators
	compression tester

Automatic Transmission:	torque wrenches
	pressure gauge 300 psi
	30—inch hg. vacuum gauge
	tachometer
	transmission jack

Manual Transmission and Rear Axle:	gear puller, axle puller
	gear press, bearing press
	dial indicator
	torque wrenches
	arbor/hydraulic press

Diagnostic Lane:	headlight alignment tester
	wheel alignment rack or tables
	brake tester
	chassis dynamometer
	diagnostic console with scope
	HC/CO (high and low scale)
	starting system and charging
	system capability
	vehicle lift, wheel spinner

OTHER CONSIDERATIONS

Does the shop have free or minimum-charge loaners, a pickup and delivery service, or a courtesy van? Is it located near a bus stop? These things could be important if you need transportation to get to and from work.

When you take a car to a garage you're usually in a bad frame of mind. I don't know of many people who are happy because their car isn't running right! Don't take your frustrations out on the mechanic. He didn't cause—I hope—your car to break down.

If it isn't an emergency, it's a good idea to have some small things done first. How you are treated getting a minor service or repair might be an indication of how you will be treated on big ticket jobs.

Don't be surprised if a shop refuses to work on your car, especially if it's a new, computer-controlled one. Many shops just don't have the know-how or equipment to diagnose and repair these cars. You should feel fortunate the shop was honest. It's better to look for another shop than to have someone experiment. But, a shop that is honest enough to admit they can't do certain kinds of work could be a good one to take your car to for work they can do.

Repair garage owners take note: One thing that bothered my wife in some places she visited was the all-male, macho atmosphere. A men's club mentality prevailed, she complained. She was looked down on as someone who didn't know a thing about cars and was treated accordingly.

Her shop preferences based on her experiences? Dealership service departments or large chain stores and independents, because they usually have women working there in some capacity and, as a rule, were cleaner and more comfortable places to be. And, they didn't treat her like one of the boys.

If you owned a business and an obnoxious customer came in, wouldn't you be tempted to pick out one of your shoddier pieces of merchandise and pawn it off on him? Wouldn't you be tempted to be a little less diligent in doing the work requested or perhaps even jiggle something here and there to make the job a bit more expensive?

Rude and obnoxious people get their own rewards. And they deserve them. Demanding that work be done now or letting the owner know how important you are, are hard-to-ignore signals. Even the most upright operator has to be tempted to fudge a little. Why open a Pandora's box of mechanics' revenge? Why not be courteous and considerate? It can only do you and your car a lot of good.

It won't take long to realize that all repair shops are not the same. It's rare to find one that can work on every kind of car. Many independents are selective, some work only on domestic cars, others on imports.

Checking out a shop or shops in advance is beneficial because you can unhurriedly appraise them and not be under any pressure while doing it. Your judgement isn't clouded by the urgency of a "must" repair.

4

Engine Analyzers

Two pieces of equipment a full-service shop should have are a computer-engine analyzer and a hand-held scan tool. Because engine analyzers and scan tools differ greatly in their accuracy, I have devoted this chapter to showing you how to pick a shop with accurate ones.

Scan tools are hand-held diagnostic devices that interface with the car's engine computer controls (Engine Control Module [ECM] or On-Board Computer [OBC]) and give the technician a readout of the trouble or fault codes, computer codes that identify the engine problem area(s).

One important determination customers should make for themselves is whether the shop has a scan tool that can read the fault codes on their car. This is important, because some scan tools aren't capable of interfacing with and "talking" to a car's computer for each and every make and model. And, for competent repair of modern computer-controlled cars, reliable chit-chat between the scan tool and the computer is vital.

In today's rapidly changing repair environment an accurate engine analyzer is required to properly diagnose modern engine system faults. An analyzer can be of inestimable help for both the experienced and novice technician in ferreting out problems. Computer-engine analyzers that have programmed software systems and "think like we do," are an even better consumer's edge in the quest to get good competent diagnosis and repair of engine system problems. In the end, you get a better repair in less time for less money.

Quality computer engine analyzers can accurately diagnose the following engine systems: starting (cranking) and charging systems, primary and secondary ignition systems, timing system, fuel system, and cylinder power and balance analysis.

Engine analyzers have been around in various forms for some time and the advent of sophisticated computers has greatly increased their potential for helping a mechanic solve both easy and tough problems in various engine systems. But just how good are the new generation of engine analyzers? Can they really make a difference in the shop? Can they overcome or at least lessen the diagnostic challenges which are growing in number and formidability as cars become more complex? Are all analyzers pretty much alike?

At a large repair facility in Pensacola, Florida, I paid $35 for a computer engine analysis of my 1984 Oldsmobile. I watched, as the impressive-looking machine went through its routine. After about a half-hour, the analyzer produced a printout noting that I had a number of problems ranging from the ignition system to fuel system to low cylinder power.

But I knew the car only had one problem, a loose spark plug wire. Why was the computer indicating other faults, and why in some other shops did the analyzers fail to find my simple problem?

Had I heeded the analyzer's (and thus, the mechanic's) suggestions, the simple correction could have become an expensive, unnecessary parts and labor bill. Surely it was an easy "find" for any scope. The answer was hidden somewhere: incompetent, inexperienced, or dishonest mechanics; unfamiliarity with or difficulty operating the analyzers or interpreting their results; or—importantly —incorrect, vague, or misleading diagnosis by the machines themselves.

A customer comes to a shop with a complaint. An engine analysis finds some bad plugs and a rich carburetor. The car is tuned, and the customer is sent on his way. But, if the analyzer can't perform an integrated test with the car's on-board computer, it can't detect a computer system's problem, and the customer returns to the garage dissatisfied with the tune-up. An integrated test would have spotted the trouble on the first visit. Net result: a happier customer and no comeback for the shop. In today's computer-engine-controlled environment, an engine analyzer that can't simultaneously test the on-board computer, just like the scan tool that is incapable of interfacing with your car's computer, is limited.

WHEN IS A RIGHT ANSWER WRONG?

Many current computer-engine analyzers use a shot-gun approach and fire a dizzying array of possible solutions at the technician. Worse, these laundry lists often don't even include some of the actual problems. Common answers such as "valve-train problem" or "secondary ignition problem" can leave even an experienced technician groping and shuffling through service manuals for more information.

It's not easy for today's automotive technician to keep up. Many don't live near a technical school or have time or money to invest in training. But without proper training, they are soon left behind. With a quality engine analyzer, he need be less concerned with keeping up, for much of the needed information, including computer-controlled component data, is stored in the analyzer's software. The best on-the-market computer-engine analyzers, in my opinion, employ such expert system technology.

EXPERT SYSTEMS

What is an expert system? It's a software package that gives a machine the ability to solve problems by mimicking the way an expert or group of experts would do it. First, the experts gather as much information as possible; then, drawing from that corpus, narrow the possibilities down to the most probable solution. If you think about it, that's how we solve a problem. First, the mind accumulates data, then it logically sifts through the bits and pieces and comes up with a solution.

MACHINES THAT THINK LIKE WE DO

A good diagnostician or mechanic likewise approaches a problem in a logical manner. First he gathers information and then tries to solve his puzzle. If he is still stumped he will go back, bone up some more, and try again. That's exactly what an expert-system-based engine analyzer does. If at first it doesn't succeed, it backs up, gathers more data, and tries again but at a much higher rate of speed.

An expert system, such as in Allen's Smart Engine Analyzer (SEA) and Smart Scope, contains the knowledge of many experts (Fig. 4-1). They logged into the system virtually every solution to nearly all engine problems. It's like having a group of expert mechanics diagnose a car. Of course, the precision and thoroughness

Fig. 4-1. The Allen Smart Engine Analyzer (SEA).

of an expert system is dependent on the experts' knowledge. On the SEA for instance, six years of research went into programming the expert system software that is refined and added to yearly.

Other engine analyzers use flow charts or trouble trees (right out of the service manuals) and compare the car's current specifications with the manufacturer's. Although this works to a limited degree, it can lead the operator to many dead ends (I've seen much evidence of this) and drastically limits the analyzer's capabilities. Our mind doesn't use flow chart patterns when it thinks, rather, it approaches the problem in a logical, information-gathering manner.

The ability to make inferential leaps—emulating the thinking process of a human being—is the single most important distinguishing factor of a true expert system. Because comparators (nonexpert systems) lack this capability, their processes are both inefficient and time consuming.

The number of diagnostic messages a system provides is a clue to its thoroughness. While other brands have totals of 87 and 102 respectively, Allen's Smart Scope and SEA each have over 500. What those numbers mean, in essence, is that they can identify 400+ more problems than their competitors, problems the others don't even acknowledge or lump under all-inclusive answers. To any keen—and not so keen—observer, those numbers carry a convincing message.

ALL ENGINE ANALYZERS AREN'T CREATED EQUAL

I took a rental car to three separate shops in Arizona, each with a different brand computer-engine analyzer. After confirming that the rental car (a 1987 Plymouth Reliant with a 2.2 liter fuel-injected engine and 18,800 miles) was in sound condition, I bugged it with a loose alternator belt, a spark plug with a very narrow gap, and a disconnected vacuum line.

The results were one-sided: the shop with the Allen SEA found all three problems while the other two found only the bad plug. One erroneously faulted the voltage regulator and primary coil resistance and questioned the engine's basic timing. When it singled out the suspect spark plug, it also asked the technician to check the distributor-cap terminal and the plug wire, a mini, but superfluous shopping list.

The other said simply: "Spark plug gap is too small, cylinder number 4." Accurate, but it ignored the other two problems.

While spec-comparing analyzers have the ability to spot simple isolated problems, it is my observation that they are easily sidetracked when dealing with multiple symptoms—especially in the same engine system. I wasn't encouraged, and neither would a customer, that the technician's operating the analyzers had doubts about their ability.

I, at one time, had the impression—as I'm certain many repair shop owners and their customers still do—that all engine analyzers were about the same. But that's far from the truth. If there's one maxim a shop owner or a car owner can hang his hat on, it's this: all engine analyzers are not created equal.

5

Effective Communication with the Technician

Complete and effective communication between the customer and repair facility is the key to a healthy relationship. A prerequisite is an understanding of what the consumer's rights are so he or she knows what to expect from the repair facility.

—Martin Dyer
Chief of the California Bureau of Automotive Repair

Effective communication starts the moment you tell the technician what's wrong with your car. Describe the symptoms in detail. The more information you can give, the better. Don't leave anything out. Be as accurate as you can. Remember the senses: sight, smell, feel, and sound. Explain any symptoms that relate to each. Does it go tick-tick or thump-thump, pull to the right or to the left? Does it happen when you start the car on a cold morning or only when the engine is hot? Does engine or car speed influence its intensity? Is is sporadic or ongoing? When did you first notice it? Where are the noises coming from? Are there odors such as gasoline or other fluids, burning rubber or plastic? Are all the gauges at or near their normal readings? Did the "check engine" light come on? You don't have to be an expert to describe symptoms.

But unless you are an expert, never try to diagnose your own problem. Let the shop do that. More often than not, a customer's diagnosis that is acted on by a technician will lead to other problems and end up costing more money in the long run. Tell the shop the symptoms and let them make the diagnosis. After all, isn't that why you took the car there?

Always try to speak directly to the person who will be working on your car. If necessary, go on a test drive with him and point out the trouble. A good shop will test drive the car both before and after any costly repair.

One of the main customer complaints about repair shops is that the work is not done right the first time. Much of this dissatisfaction can be traced to the fact that some shops are so busy, so large, so impersonal, that the customer never gets a chance to talk to the technician who will be working on his or her car. A lot of important information gets lost in the shuffle between the customer and the mechanic when a service writer is employed as the middleman. Many service writers are harried, pressed for time, and are almost forced to abbreviate.

Your detailed explanation might end up as "engine runs rough" or "front end noise." This doesn't give the mechanic much meat to sink his teeth into, and he is sometimes forced to experiment—on your time—to find things you initially told the service writer. You can combat this inefficiency by providing the shop with a written list of symptoms in addition to the verbal one. Give it to the service writer and request that it be stapled to your work order, or hand deliver it yourself to the technician who will be working on your car.

Some new car manufacturers are taking steps to alleviate this communication gap. Chevrolet's Master Repair Program encourages service writers to give detailed accounts of the customer's complaint, and mechanics are paid for the extra time it takes to diagnose a problem properly before attempting repairs. Ford and Chrysler pay the technician for the extra time situations after he explains in writing why the time was needed.

If someone has recommended a mechanic to you, request that he work on your car. If you have more confidence in a certain technician, ask that he does the repair. One of the shops on my *Reader's Recommended Mechanics List* was a new car dealer's service department. The reader recommending it did so because he liked a certain mechanic working there. He specified that any interested party should ask for that technician.

If you don't communicate effectively the technician might have to spend extra time at your expense finding out things you could have told him to begin with. What might seem trivial to you now could be the exact clue a technician needs later. A technician is like a doctor: the more you can tell him about what is ailing you, the faster and cheaper it is for him to get you well.

We live in an age of fast food, quick lubes, and packaged convenience. When we go to a mechanic some of that mentality tags along. We want our cars fixed right now if not sooner. You shouldn't expect a mechanic to drop what he is doing to start work on your car. Remember, you might need your car, but so do the customers ahead of you.

It always pays to be courteous, friendly, and patient. When we broke down in Las Cruces, it was because of our patient and considerate attitude, we later found out, that the service writer and manager went out of their way to help.

When talking to the technician, don't try to judge his ability or honesty by his looks or the way he talks or dresses. I've tried it many times. It just doesn't work.

Here's a neat idea suggested by Sonja Freidman, when I appeared on her CNN show, "Sonja in LA." A prospective shop customer says something like this to the technician: "I know you are honest. I trust you and know you will treat me fairly and do a good job. My car is important to me. Please don't disappoint me." Talk about communicating effectively! This direct approach spells out your expectations and virtually obligates the shop to be fair. It sure won't do any harm trying it.

If you happen to catch a mechanic on his lunch or coffee break, cool your heels. One technician told me that when someone interrupts his lunch or coffee break, he makes sure they pay for his inconvenience somewhere on the bill.

Don't be afraid to compliment a technician on a job well done, even if it means making a special trip to the shop at some later date. Everyone appreciates a compliment. Me, I make sure my mechanic gets a Christmas gift each year.

FAIL-SAFE AUTO REPAIR PROTECTION: GETTING A SECOND OPINION

One of the most important pieces of advice this book can give is: when in doubt, get a second opinion. If the estimate seems high or you have reason to question the shop's diagnosis, take the car to another shop and get a second opinion and estimate. We commonly do this with doctors, why not repair shops? If the repair appears to be an expensive one the difference in estimates can sometimes be considerable. But money isn't the only reason you want to get another opinion and estimate.

The second opinion could differ from the first. For example, the first shop says you need a valve job and estimates the cost at $500. But a second shop's diagnosis indicates your only problem is a broken valve spring and gives you a $95 estimate. Obviously, you want the second shop to be right, and it's likely you will go with their diagnosis.

Sometimes, it might even pay to get a third opinion if the first two conflict. When two shops agree on the kind and amount of work you need, chances are excellent that both diagnoses are correct.

Whatever you do don't bias a subsequent shop's diagnosis by telling them what another shop said. You don't want their opinion to be influenced by another shop's diagnosis. Just tell them what is wrong with the car and let them do the search. After receiving a second or even third opinion, you can now choose the shop you feel is best.

Although getting a second or third opinion is time consuming, it is one of the best ways to insure you are getting the proper repair at a fair price. Of course, one wouldn't want to spend all day running around town trying to get a better price on a $35 repair, but it sure might be worth your while if the first estimate is tickling three or four figures.

When we purchase expensive carpeting or a major appliance for our homes, we shop around until we find the best deal on price, quality, and service. Do the same with expensive car repair. Get a second or even third opinion and estimate.

A customer is sometimes put in the spotlight when a shop suggests a big dollar repair. Some are embarrassed to "just say no." They don't want to tell the mechanic that they're going to go to another shop for a second opinion. These Casper Milktoasts are ideal fodder for a rip-off's cannon: not being able to make the decision they should, customers yield to their meek sides and open the door to unneeded repairs.

You can also take the car to a diagnostic center for an evaluation. The technicians will go over your car with a fine-tooth-diagnostic comb and offer a written opinion on what is wrong with it and what it will take to fix it. The cost varies, but it is currently around $40 to $70. These diagnostic shops don't do repair work so it doesn't matter to them whether your car needs repair or not. In essence, they are disinterested parties. Their opinion can reinforce a repair shop's. If the repair shop's opinion is at odds with the diagnostic shop's opinion, you would be wise to go to another shop.

6

Codes of Ethics

It always makes me feel good when I see a code of ethics hanging on a shop wall. Just the idea that the owner went through the trouble to place it there tells me that he is trying to conduct his business by some set of ground rules. Of course, a code of ethics is only as good as the person's resolve to abide by it. A shop could put it there as a lure to attract customers and then "take them to the cleaners" once trust is established. But in the shops I visited that displayed a code, that wasn't the case. Read the code, see what it says, and hold the shop to it. If the shop displays it, they should abide by it, and you should take advantage of it.

Below is the code of ethics of the Automotive Service Association (ASA), the largest trade group of technicians in the country. Look at some of the voluntary standards they have set for their member shops:

- To perform high quality repair service at a fair and just price.
- To use only proven merchandise of high quality distributed by reputable firms.
- To employ the best skilled technicians obtainable.
- To furnish an itemized invoice that clearly identifies any used or remanufactured parts for fairly priced parts and services. Replaced parts can be inspected upon request.
- To have a sense of personal obligation to each individual customer.

- To promote good will between the motorist and members of this association.
- To recommend corrective and maintenance services, explaining to the customer which of these are required to correct existing problems and which are for preventive maintenance.
- To offer the customer a price estimate for work to be performed.
- To furnish or post copies of any warranties covering parts or services.
- To obtain prior authorization for all work done, in writing or by other means satisfactory to the customer.
- To notify the customer if appointments or completion promises cannot be kept.
- To maintain customer service records for one year or more.
- To exercise reasonable care for the customer's property while in our possession.
- To maintain a system for fair settlement of customer's complaints.
- To cooperate with established consumer complaint-mediation activities.
- To uphold the high standards of our profession and always seek to correct any and all abuses within the automotive industry.
- To uphold the integrity of all members of the Automotive Service Association.

The California Automotive Service Councils (ASC), an affiliate of ASA, adds another tenet to their code, and in my opinion, it's an important one:

- To refrain from advertisement which is false or misleading or likely to confuse or deceive the customer.

Wouldn't it be nice if all repair shops abided by these rules? Indeed, if you find a shop that will honor each and every promise made above, your battle is practically won. But regardless of how good you feel about a particular shop, no matter how many of the recommendations we make are found there, the proof will be in how they treat you and your car. The prices they charge, the quality of work they provide, how their work is guaranteed, how they handle comebacks—all these and more will tell you whether or not to go back again.

But how about the customer? Doesn't he or she have some responsibilities? Is this just a one-way street with the shop owners and technicians bearing the brunt of the ethical load? It shouldn't be.

Why not a customer code of ethics? A set of rules by which the customer should abide when having his or her car repaired? Here are some suggestions:

A REPAIR SHOP CUSTOMER'S CODE OF ETHICS

- I will not expect a technician to work for free, even if only for a few minutes. His time is as valuable as mine.
- I expect to pay for diagnosis of my problem, whether or not the diagnostic shop is the one that does the repair.
- I will treat the owner and his employees with the same respect and courtesy that I expect.
- I am aware that if the shop is busy, they won't be able to work on my car "right now."
- I won't sabotage work done to make it look shoddy in an attempt to get my money back.
- I won't bother a technician while he is working on a car, unless he requests my presence or I ask first.
- I know that even the best technician can make an honest mistake.
- I will call ahead for an appointment when possible.
- I will make sure my car is ready before I go to the shop to pick it up.
- I will pick up my car when it is ready and not expect the shop to babysit.
- I will notify the shop when the work order is made out how I intend to pay for the job.
- I won't rely on the shop to provide transportation, in the event my car is tied up for a long time.
- If the work should prove unsatisfactory, I will return the car to the shop as soon as possible.

Now you're not going to find that list posted in any repair shop, but it wouldn't be a bad idea to review it each time you get ready to take your car in for servicing or repair.

7

Trade Organizations, Certification and "Approved" Repairs

As you look for a repair facility no doubt you will come across one or more of the "A" signs. They might be displayed outside or inside the shop or even on the technician's sleeves. What are these "A" signs, and are they indications of a quality repair shop?

A signs are my way of designating a number of trade organizations, certification groups, and approved auto repair shops. Their acronyms usually begin with an "A" and most always stands for Automotive or Automobile.

Four good examples of "A" signs are ASE (Automotive Service Excellence), ASA (Automotive Service Association), ASC (Automotive Service Councils), and AAA (American Automobile Association). Let's look at these organizations to see how and if they can help a consumer in need of auto repair.

AAA APPROVED AUTO REPAIR: THE ONLY NATIONAL AUTO REPAIR SHOP MONITORING SYSTEM

A select number of repair shops sport the AAA APPROVED AUTO REPAIR sign. You do not have to be a member of AAA to frequent these shops. Is it a sign of better and honest service? A brochure from AAA explains and answers questions about AAA approved auto repair:

Fig. 7-1. AAA approved auto repair sign. REPRINTED WITH PERMISSION OF AAA.

AAA has established stringent approval criteria for repair facilities in the areas of manpower, equipment, facility appearance, customer service, community reputation, and scope of service. The technically competent program coordinator conducts a rigorous inspection of facilities seeking AAA approval. Following the completion of the investigation and inspection of the repair facility, an AAA Review Board evaluates the facility and makes a decision regarding granting approval. If the Review Board's decision is favorable, the repair facility is offered a contract. The repair facility must agree to accept all provisions of the contract, guarantee its workmanship, and abide by AAA's decision in settling a dispute between an AAA member and the Approved Facility. Members can recognize approved facilities by the red, white, and blue Approved Auto Repair sign displayed outside on the premises and the Certificate of Approval displayed inside in the customer waiting area.

Some of the key paragraphs in the Approved Auto Repair Services Program Contract also show what a customer can expect from one of these facilities:

■   "The Approved Facility will . . . maintain and have available sufficient personnel and appropriate equipment to render, by appointment, an acceptable diagnosis and repair service during regular business hours to any member who requests such services and presents a valid membership card provided such diagnosis or repair is within the

Approved Facility's areas of expertise . . . . All buildings, including adequate waiting room and rest room facilities, grounds, equipment, and personnel of the Approved Facility shall be clean, neat-appearing, and of a caliber satisfactory and acceptable to AAA.

■   "Prior to initiating any diagnostic or repair work, the Approved Facility must offer to provide the AAA member with a written estimate indicating work required, cost, and completion date. In the event detailed diagnosis or disassembly is required in order to make an accurate estimate, the charges for such work including reassembly, where applicable, shall be disclosed to the member prior to engaging in such activity. The Approved Facility shall receive written authorization from the AAA member to make repairs on the basis of the written estimate. The AAA member may, by signature, waive his right to a written estimate and agree instead to a verbal estimate. Where it is found that the work required will exceed the written or verbal estimate, the Approved Facility agrees to comply with state or local laws regarding repair estimates. But in any event, it must secure written or verbal authorization from the AAA member if the work required exceeds the estimate by ten (10) percent.

■   "The Approved Facility has the right to refuse to accept a particular job, especially if it could be of a complex nature. However, once the repair has started, it must see to it that the repair is carried though speedily to a satisfactory conclusion. The Approved Facility will acquaint itself with recommended maintenance procedures for each vehicle it accepts for repairs, and will work in accordance with these procedures.

■   "The Approved Facility must guarantee the effectiveness of repairs, parts, or components for 90 days or 4,000 miles under normal operating conditions. If due to the age or condition of the vehicle, there is risk that the repair may not be wholly satisfactory, the AAA member must be advised as soon as this is determined. This must be documented in writing.

■   "The Approved Facility agrees to make available any replaced parts after the repairs are completed except parts required to be returned to the manufacturer or distributor under a warranty agreement. However, these parts must be available for inspection by the AAA member. The Approved Facility agrees to install new parts unless specific authorization to install used or rebuilt parts is obtained from the member. The invoice must state if used, rebuilt, or reconditioned parts were installed. The shop will not use additives to motor oil or gasoline without the member's consent. A copy of the invoice must be given to the AAA member upon payment of service.

■   "The Approved Facility agrees that in the event of a member's complaint to the AAA, it will cooperate fully in any investigation thereof. In the event of a dispute between the member and the shop as to whether repairs authorized by the member have been properly completed, an AAA representative shall have the right to inspect any work, materials, and charges and to inspect and obtain copies of diagnostic and repair records, invoices, or other records pertinent to the dispute and conduct such tests as he deems necessary. Thereafter he shall report the results of the investigation in writing to the Approved Facility and the member. In the event he concludes that repairs have been improperly completed, the Approved Facility shall satisfactorily complete the repairs or refund the charge therefore to the member. The costs of the investigation and tests made by the AAA shall be borne by the AAA."

When the repair facility signs a contract with AAA it also agrees to abide by AAA's decision in any dispute with any AAA member.

Although the above paragraphs refer to one of the parties as an "AAA member," let's emphasize again that you do not have to be a member of AAA to use an AAA approved repair shop. Just like non-AAA members can go to an AAA approved motel, so can they use an approved repair shop. However, a nonmember will not have AAA's assistance in case of a dispute with the repair facility.

FACILITY SERVICE EVALUATION

Please fill out, detach and mail to (AAA) (Check only one box per question)

	EXCELLENT	GOOD	FAIR	POOR	1 YES	2 NO
1. How would you rate this facility overall?	☐	☐	☐	☐		
2. Was the estimate for work to be done adhered to or if additional work was required, were you consulted?					☐	☐
3. Was the repair work done to your satisfaction?					☐	☐
4. Were the personnel knowledgeable, courteous, and efficient?					☐	☐
5. Was the car ready when promised?					☐	☐
6. Have you ever used this repair facility in the past?					☐	☐
7. Would you return to this facility in the future?					☐	☐
8. Were you aware that this was an (AAA) Approved Auto Repair Facility?					☐	☐
9. Are you a member of the American Automobile Association?					☐	☐

NAME OF FACILITY	REPAIR ORDER NO.
YOUR NAME	MEMBERSHIP NO.
HOME PHONE WORK PHONE	
COMMENTS:	

38-8058 (8/86)

Fig. 7-2. AAA facility evaluation card. REPRINTED WITH PERMISSION OF AAA.

AAA Approved Auto Repair ■ 45

MONITORING THE APPROVED SHOPS

After a vehicle is repaired, the customer is asked to rate the overall repair experience by filling out a questionnaire card about the shop and the repair. The customer, and not the shop, mails the card to the AAA where each is evaluated. Each month AAA then issues a report to the shops showing the shops how they compare to others in the approved program. It's the only national monitoring program of its kind.

What we see in the AAA credo of Approved Auto Repair are many of the exact things we've told the reader to look for when seeking auto repair. The AAA program is an ambitious one and is, in my mind, on the right track. But to keep a handle on all its shops, the AAA must keep the number of approved shops small so they can be monitored by the various AAA sectors. Looking for the AAA Approved Auto Repair sign, however, is another consumer's edge in the auto repair jungle.

CERTIFICATION: DOES IT MEAN BETTER REPAIRS?

The National Institute for Automotive Service Excellence (ASE) is a nonprofit corporation that promotes the "highest standards of automotive service in the public interest." Through a voluntary com-

Fig. 7-3. ASE certified sign.

petency testing and certification program, it measures and recognizes the diagnostic and repair skills of automobile and heavy-duty truck technicians, as well as body repairers and painters.

Certification tests for technicians are held twice a year at over 300 locations across the country. Before a mechanic is eligible for certification, he must have a minimum of two years work experience as a technician. Currently, tests are offered in engine repair; automatic transmission/transaxle; manual drive train and axles; suspension and steering; brakes; electrical systems; heating and air conditioning, and engine performance. In addition, other tests are offered for heavy-duty truck technicians and auto body repairers and painters.

Persons who pass these tests can wear certified badges proclaiming their areas of competency. They have achieved, in ASE's eyes, enough proficiency in a particular repair field to become certified. A technician who passes all tests is designated as a Certified Master Technician. To remain certified in any area, the technician must pass tests every 5 years.

ASE certified technicians can be found most everywhere. ASE is the largest certifying agency in the country, and currently there are about 200,000 ASE technicians in the repair marketplace. With that many certified technicians it isn't hard to find a shop that employs one. Blue and white ASE signs proclaim that the shop uses at least one certified technician.

But remember, you can't certify honesty. Belonging to an organization is no guarantee that a shop or technician is honest. In my cross-country check of repair facilities, certified technicians were found to be no more honest than others. But certification does show that the mechanic has spent the time, money, and effort to learn about a subject and to voluntarily take and pass the certifying tests.

Even though a shop displays a certified sign, the customer should determine: if the technician's credentials are up to date—they should be posted in the office of waiting room—if the certified mechanic will be the one working on your car, and if he is certified in the area of car repair needed. It doesn't help if a mechanic is wearing a brake-certified patch when you are in need of transmission repair. Remember, one certified sign does not indicate that all the mechanics in the shop are certified.

TRADE ORGANIZATIONS

The Automotive Service Association (ASA) and the California Automotive Service Councils (ASC) are two of the most prominent repair industry trade organizations. Are shops that display these or other trade organization logos a better deal for the consumer?

Belonging to a trade group helps a shop in a number of ways, and because the shop benefits, so does its customers. Earlier we reviewed the code of ethics of the ASA and ASC and found their principles to be those a consumer would like to see each and every shop adhere to. These self-imposed ethical standards are but one example of how a trade group can influence the behavior of its individual members.

ASA, the nation's largest trade association with over 11,000 member-shops nationwide, and its affiliate ASC, make available to members such things as new technological information and news about recent legislation effecting the auto industry; general industry news; training programs; business aids; and an in-house magazine with up-to-date helpful information and a lot more.

In addition, annual meetings and conventions for the general membership and separate meetings for its mechanical, collision, and transmission divisions, allow members to keep in touch with the latest industry developments. More importantly perhaps, these get-togethers allow members frequent opportunities to foster new relationships and exchange ideas to improve the quality of service they offer.

ASA's president, Allen Richey, says that ASA's "independent automotive service facilities are dedicated to providing the highest quality automotive repair at a fair and just price. ASA aims to advance the prestige of the automotive service industry through the promotion of the highest ethical standards, education, and legislation when necessary."

Although any type of certification or membership to a trade association is desirable, it should never be the only reason for choosing a shop or technician. I've heard stories about mechanics who couldn't pass a written test but could tear down and fix an engine or transmission blindfolded. There are many capable technicians working in the marketplace who don't belong to any organization.

8

The Work Order and Estimate: How to Avoid the 5 o'clock Surprise

There is no worse feeling after a hard day at the office than arriving at a repair shop to pick up your car and find that—surprise!—the cheerful $50 estimate you received in the morning has ballooned into a $250 won't-go-away bad dream.

Consumers must understand what rights they have and what rightfully can be expected from a repair facility. One document spells out these expectations, and no repair, no matter how small or seemingly insignificant, should proceed without it. I'm talking about a completed written work order signed by both the car owner and the shop (Figs. 8-1, 8-2, and 8-3).

The work order should specify the exact nature and extent of the work to be done, the approximate time the job will take, the approximate cost of the repair, and what the shop should do in the event additional work or parts are needed. It should also cover if the parts are new, rebuilt, or used, if you want the old parts returned to you, and if the work and parts are guaranteed. Make sure the warranty covers the repair and leave a phone number where you can be reached.

WARRANTIES AND GUARANTEES

A customer should also understand what any written warranty covers. If any part of a car is rebuilt or repaired, a good shop will

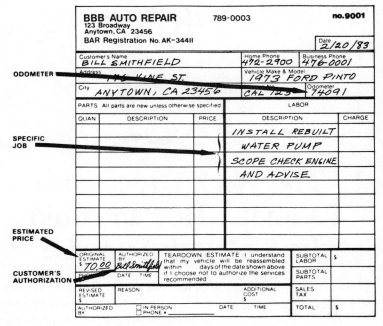

ODOMETER

SPECIFIC
JOB

ESTIMATED
PRICE

CUSTOMER'S
AUTHORIZATION

Fig. 8-1. Written estimate/work order. (California Bar).

offer a written warranty on the work and parts. According to the Federal Trade Commission the warranty should clearly state the following:

- What the warranty covers
- For what period of time or number of miles
- What exclusions or conditions apply to the coverage
- What the owner's responsibilities are for operation and maintenance, such as whether the warranty requires that the car be inspected annually
- What is required to obtain repair work under the warranty
- What the service provisions are if the part fails while the car is being driven out of town

A shop that backs its work and parts is saying to its customers that it is confident it can fix their cars right the first time.

The work order binds both the customer and the shop to its instructions. It can become important evidence in case of a dispute

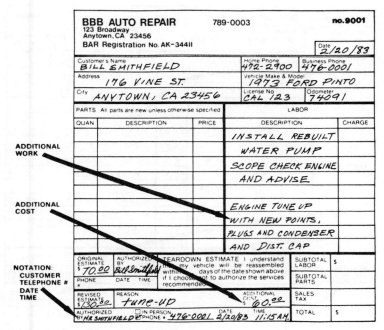

BBB AUTO REPAIR	789-0003			no.9001

BBB AUTO REPAIR 789-0003 no.9001
123 Broadway
Anytown, CA 23456
BAR Registration No. AK-344II

Date 2/20/83

Customer's Name	Home Phone	Business Phone
BILL SMITHFIELD	472-2900	476-0001

Address	Vehicle Make & Model
176 VINE ST.	1973 FORD PINTO

City	License No.	Odometer
ANYTOWN, CA 23456	CAL 123	74091

PARTS All parts are new unless otherwise specified LABOR

QUAN	DESCRIPTION	PRICE	DESCRIPTION	CHARGE
			INSTALL REBUILT	
			WATER PUMP	
			SCOPE CHECK ENGINE	
			AND ADVISE	
			ENGINE TUNE UP	
			WITH NEW POINTS,	
			PLUGS AND CONDENSER	
			AND DIST. CAP	

ADDITIONAL WORK

ADDITIONAL COST

NOTATION: CUSTOMER TELEPHONE # DATE TIME

ORIGINAL ESTIMATE $ 70.00	AUTHORIZED BY Bill Smithfield	TEARDOWN ESTIMATE I understand that my vehicle will be reassembled within ___ days of the date shown above if I choose not to authorize the services recommended	SUBTOTAL LABOR $
PHONE #	DATE TIME		SUBTOTAL PARTS
REVISED ESTIMATE $ 130.00	REASON tune-up	ADDITIONAL COST $ 60.00	SALES TAX
AUTHORIZED BY MR SMITHFIELD	☐ IN PERSON ☑ PHONE # 476-0001	DATE 2/20/83 TIME 11:15 A.M.	TOTAL $

Fig. 8-2. Additional authorization. (California Bar).

arising from dissatisfaction with the repair. If the work order doesn't cover any of the above specifics they should be written in.

Be sure everything is correct before you sign a work order. If the estimate seems high or if you question the shop's diagnosis, don't sign it. Take the car to another shop for a second opinion on the kind and amount of work needed.

Once you are satisfied that the work order/estimate is complete, you and the shop representative should sign it. Don't forget to get your copy. Insist on it, for if you don't, there is nothing to prevent a service dealer from adding extra work or parts to the list. A work order protects and benefits both the shop and the customer, and a good establishment will always offer one to its customers.

I received a letter from a reader of my syndicated column. The writer, a widow of 71, took her car into a service station for a tune-up. But she forgot to ask for a copy of the work order (see chapter 12). The service station took advantage of her slight by charging over $700 to fix the air conditioner, which, according to the lady, was working just fine when she took the car in. Oh yes, they did do the tune-up.

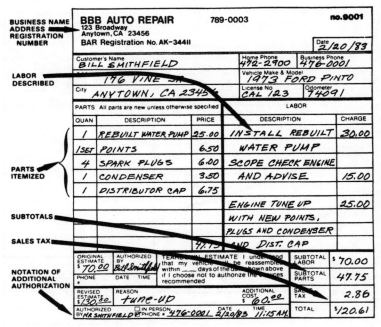

BUSINESS NAME
ADDRESS
REGISTRATION
NUMBER

LABOR
DESCRIBED

PARTS
ITEMIZED

SUBTOTALS

SALES TAX

NOTATION OF
ADDITIONAL
AUTHORIZATION

BBB AUTO REPAIR	789-0003		no.9001
123 Broadway			
Anytown, CA 23456			
BAR Registration No. AK-3441I			Date 2/20/83

Customer's Name BILL SMITHFIELD		Home Phone 472-2900	Business Phone 476-0001
176 VINE ST.		Vehicle Make & Model 1973 FORD PINTO	
City ANYTOWN, CA 23456		License No CAL 123	Odometer 74091

PARTS All parts are new unless otherwise specified — LABOR

QUAN	DESCRIPTION	PRICE	DESCRIPTION	CHARGE
1	REBUILT WATER PUMP	25.00	INSTALL REBUILT	30.00
1SET	POINTS	6.50	WATER PUMP	
4	SPARK PLUGS	6.00	SCOPE CHECK ENGINE	
1	CONDENSER	3.50	AND ADVISE	15.00
1	DISTRIBUTOR CAP	6.75		
			ENGINE TUNE UP	25.00
			WITH NEW POINTS,	
			PLUGS AND CONDENSER	
		47.75	AND DIST. CAP	

ORIGINAL ESTIMATE $ 70.00	AUTHORIZED BY Bill Smithfield	TEARDOWN ESTIMATE I understand that my vehicle will be reassembled within ____ days of the undershown above if I choose not to authorize the services recommended	SUBTOTAL LABOR	$ 70.00
PHONE	DATE TIME		SUBTOTAL PARTS	47.75
REVISED ESTIMATE $130.50	REASON tune-up	ADDITIONAL COST $ 60.00	SALES TAX	2.86
AUTHORIZED BY MR SMITHFIELD	☐ IN PERSON ☑ PHONE = 476-0001	DATE 2/20/83 TIME 11:15 A.M.	TOTAL	$120.61

Fig. 8-3. Final invoice. (California Bar).

Although verbal commitments are nice among friends, when it comes to auto repair, they can be a disaster. Put it in writing, not in the air. No matter how much you like the person you are doing business with, get it down in black and white.

At this point it should also be determined who is responsible for your vehicle in the event it becomes damaged while at the shop. Even though the damage isn't your fault the shop might not pay for, or consider itself liable for, any damage incurred to a vehicle in their possession. Determine who is responsible for what. A mechanic should note any dents or broken glass or lights so the customer doesn't later accuse him of damaging the car.

Never sign a blank work order. It's like signing a blank check. You hand the shop a carte blanche to do whatever they want at whatever price they choose. A number of shops tried to get both me and my wife to sign blank authorization forms before they started work.

Repair industry authorities emphasize over and over the importance of securing a written and signed work order/estimate. The two most frequent consumer complaints against auto repair shops are failure to give a written estimate to the customer and doing unauthorized work. Both of these improprieties can be nipped in the bud with a written work order/estimate. The work order—don't leave the shop without one and 5 o'clock won't hold any surprises for you.

AFTER THE REPAIR AND BEFORE THE BILL

Before you return to the shop to pick up your repaired or serviced vehicle, call first. Although it might have been promised at a certain time, it might not be ready. This can save you an extra trip. The shop also should have the courtesy to inform you of any delay.

Check the car while it's still at the shop to determine to the best of your ability if the promised work was actually done. Take the car for a drive to be sure the wheels don't wobble any more, or the car doesn't miss on sudden acceleration. Make sure that whatever was wrong is now corrected. It only takes a few minutes more of your time and could save you a return trip to the shop if something isn't right.

At this time the shop should return your old parts if you requested them. Many places advertise they will save old parts for your inspection, but even if they don't, ask to see them. Even though the old parts have to be sent to a rebuilder or returned to the manufacturer for warranty reasons, you can still ask to inspect them before they are shipped out. But this is no iron-clad guarantee that the parts you get are the ones that were originally on your car. What you get might not be what you had.

When I asked to see the old parts that were allegedly replaced on the *Reader's Digest* Oldsmobile, some mechanics grabbed for the nearest thing or said they threw the parts away. The fact of the matter was they never replaced the parts.

Verify as best you can that the parts returned to you are the ones that were on your car. A cheat might say he replaced an item when all he did was clean or paint the old one and charge for a new or rebuilt one. Warns Fred Pirochta, director of the Repair Facility Division of Michigan's Bureau of Automotive Regulation: "Very rarely did the customer actually get the parts back that came out of the car during our undercover Operation Shifty."

It might be hard to identify a part that was originally on your car, especially if you don't know a hill of beans about mechanical stuff. So it might be worthwhile, particularly before a long trip, to ask your mechanic or a knowledgeable friend to mark some of the most likely parts (see chapter 11 on Rip-offs) in an inconspicuous spot with a little dab of paint or permanent marker. That way you will know for sure that the old parts you got back were actually the ones on your car.

Ron Dietrick, Tucson assistant city attorney and consumer affairs supervisor, says a customer should not be afraid to go into the shop to retrieve parts if necessary. Remember, the old parts rightfully belong to you.

9

The Technician's Lament

A couple of years ago I received the following letter from an automotive technician:

Dear Bob:

    I recently attended a course in Ford computer-ignition systems. The instructor read us the enclosed poem. As an automotive technician, I think the poem is accurate in depicting the way the public views us. Please publish it in your column for all of us who work in the automotive field who don't feel that they get just compensation for their services.

Sincerely, G. L.

    I published the poem and received a lot of response, both positive and negative. I believe the poem makes a number of good points consumers should be aware of and does so with good humor. It was written by Jim Conners of Fred Frederick Chrysler-Plymouth in Laurel, Maryland. I call it "The Technician's Lament."

> I'm a journeyman technician
> In an automotive shop,
> I'm supposed to know the answers
> From the bottom to the top.
>
> I should diagnose the problem
> With just a single look,
> And if I fail to fix it
> You think that I'm a crook.

When I charge you for my labor
You yell and scream and moan,
And even call and threaten me
Upon the telephone.

But technology in the auto
Is advancing every year,
And for the systems I must know
I simply have no peer.

Electronics have now made the scene
And more are coming yet,
Some models now will far exceed
Your television set.

In hydraulics I have more to learn
Than a specialist in pumps,
There's brakes and shock absorbers
to help absorb the bumps.

Torque converters and transmissions
With servos, valves, and gears,
With models by the hundreds
Introduced in recent years.

Fuel systems of a hundred kinds
I must adjust and meter,
Each far more complicated
Than your furnace or water heater.

I'm in welding, I'm in plumbing
For water, vacuum, oil, and fuel,
Compared to me, a plumber
Is a kid in grammar school.

There's alignment and there's balancing
And God alone knows what,
If I fix it, that's expected
If I don't, I'm on the spot.

There's models, makes, and systems
Some 700 strong,
And new ones coming up each year
To help the scheme along.

Now compare me to a doctor
Whose prices make mine meager,
Yet folks revere his expertise
Ever more impressed and eager.

The human body hasn't changed
In 20,000 years,
And every model works the same
From the ankles to the ears.

There's new equipment and techniques
And medicines for sure,
But this is true in my field too
As much, or even more.

There's lots of books he has to read
His procedures to define,
But for every page in his field
There's 25 in mine.

There's no comebacks and no warranty
You pay for what you get,
And then come back and pay again
If he hasn't fixed it yet.

His mistakes are often buried
While mine come back for free.
And he plays golf on Wednesday
While my customers hassle me.

We spend millions of tax dollars
Sending kids to medical school.
But if you ask for some in my field
You're treated like a fool.

Everybody has one body
No one has more.
But when it comes to autos
You may have three or four.

But you'll go right on complaining
Of the way I run my show,
With no appreciation
For the things I have to know.

And you'll take your high school dropouts
And shove them off to us,
And expect them to be experts
While you rant and rave and fuss.

And when your car cannot be serviced
I'll not hang my head in shame.
So you'd best wake up America
And find out who's to blame.

10

When it's Time
to Pay the Bill

When it's time to pay the tab it's smart to use a check or credit card instead of cash. There are a number of reasons for this. Paying by check gives you a time cushion to stop payment in case the repair proves faulty. Paying with cash should be your last resort. According to the Federal Trade Commission's Bureau of Consumer Protection, paying for auto repairs with a credit card is the best way.

Did you ever think about using a credit card as a protection against faulty or unnecessary auto repairs? Using a credit card instead of cash can save the day for a consumer who is having problems with an auto mechanic, says the FTC.

Suppose you take your car to the mechanic because of a noise in the power steering. The shop does a rack-and-pinion overhaul. You pay $180 with your credit card and drive home. The next afternoon, the noise is back. Another mechanic looks at the car and finds that the real problem was fluid leaking from the power steering pump. That will cost another $125 to repair.

What happens if the first mechanic refuses to make good on his mistake? If you had paid the bill with cash, you would be out $180 and might have to file suit to recover payment. Payment with a credit card not only gives you extra time, but is also an effective tool for negotiating with the mechanic.

According to federal law, if you have a problem with goods or services purchased with your credit card, you have the same legal rights in dealing with the credit card issuer as you have with the auto mechanic. In other words, because you have the right to withhold payment from the auto mechanic for sloppy or incorrect repairs, you also have the right to refuse to pay the credit card company. Of course, you may withhold no more than the amount of the repair in dispute.

In order to use this important right, you must first try to work things out with the auto mechanic. Also, unless the card issuer owns or operates the repair shop (this might be true if your car is repaired at a gas station and you use a gasoline credit card), two other conditions must be met:

■ The auto mechanic's shop must be in your home state or, if not in your state, within 100 miles of your current address.
■ The cost of repairs must be over $50.

You can hold onto your money until the dispute is settled or resolved in court. The credit card company cannot make you pay interest or other penalty charges on the amount you are withholding until that time.

If you decide not to pay, the FTC advises that you send a letter to both the credit card company and the auto mechanic. Include the date of repair, the credit card used, your account number, why the service was unsatisfactory, and what you want in settlement of your dispute. It is a good idea to send the letter by certified mail with a return receipt requested.

This law was designed to protect you. Using it will put you in a good bargaining position with both time and money on your side. Many disputes will be settled at this point, with one side or both sides compromising to reach a settlement. Some will not be.

Sometimes the credit card company or the auto mechanic will take action to put a bad mark on your credit record because you did not pay your bill. You might not be reported as delinquent, but a creditor can report that you are disputing a charge. For this reason, you should know your rights under the Fair Credit Reporting Act.

This act permits you to learn what information is in your credit file and to challenge any information you feel is incorrect. If the credit bureau cannot prove the information is true, they have to remove it. You also have the right to have your side of the story added to your file.

The mechanic may also feel strongly enough to go to court to

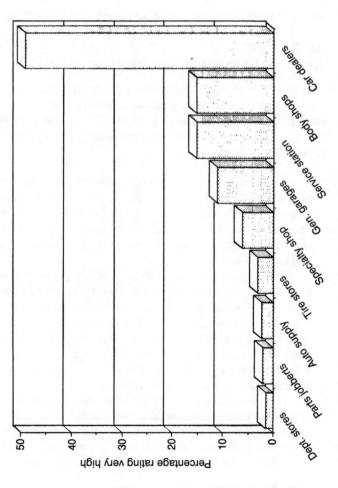

Fig. 10-1. Rate the automotive outlets by the price they charge.

collect his bill. If this happens, you will probably want to talk to a lawyer to make sure you are on solid legal ground.

Using a credit card will not solve all your auto repair problems. But it is a tool to use in tough negotiations. And auto repair complaints are among society's toughest.

You get what you pay for, goes the old saying, but is that true when it comes to auto repairs? Many times the price of a repair is influenced by the amount of overhead a shop has. That's probably why dealer service departments are usually more expensive than independents. They must charge more—and so must other shops in high rent districts—to make up for the higher wages they pay mechanics, for higher prices they pay for parts, and for the extra money it takes just to keep a large organization functioning.

AUTO SERVICE CONTRACTS: ARE THEY AN ANSWER TO YOUR REPAIR BLUES?

The Federal Trade Commission has a one-page document that answers questions about auto service contracts. Because this is a subject that involves auto repair, it is reprinted to answer questions about these devices that might or might not save you money on your auto repair bills.

A major service contract company advertises its contracts as: "The inflation-beater . . . for pennies a day you can have peace of mind." The appeal to pocketbook and the promise of "no hassle" are undeniably effective. An estimated 50% of new car buyers purchase service contracts. Are these consumers making a wise choice?

While new cars come with a "free" warranty provided by the manufacturer, a service contract is different from a warranty. A *service contract* provides a specific time during which the service contractor agrees to repair or maintain your car for an agreed-upon price. You purchase it separately from the car and don't have to buy it from the dealer. Your car may not have to be defective to get service, either. The service contract could be for routine inspection and maintenance only.

How do you know whether a service contract is a good deal? Each case is different, and only you can decide. To make a smart decision you need to read and understand the contract— before you purchase it. Here are some questions to keep in mind:

Who is responsible for the contract? If a company that offers service contracts lacks funds or insurance and goes out of business, it may not be able to repay claims. If this happens, you will be stuck with a worthless piece of paper.

Many dealers offer their own contracts on new and used cars. Most of these dealers have independent service contract companies administering their service contract program. While some dealers set aside funds or buy insurance to cover future claims, others don't. Even if the dealer has a service contract company administer the program, you should find out if that company, or an insurance company, will honor your contract if the dealer goes out of business.

Some car makers also offer service contracts, generally covering only new cars. These service contracts are frequently sold through dealers or through mailings from the manufacturer.

What is covered? A service contract may cover all major systems of the car or only some of them. Some dealers and manufacturers offer a choice of plans—from the least expensive covering a few systems to the most expensive covering many systems. Also, a service contract may cover all the parts in those systems, or it may cover only the expensive problems. Sometimes a potentially expensive repair is excluded. You should assume that the contract doesn't cover anything resulting from misuse or failure to maintain the car.

Aside from repair costs, some contracts have full or partial towing and rental reimbursement coverage. Be sure to see how much these contracts cover.

What will my service contract give me that my warranty won't? Your warranty coverage and your service contract may overlap for a year or so. If they do, you should compare the coverages and decide whether the additional expenses for the added coverage of the service contract is worth it.

How will my repair bills be paid? Your service contract company may pay the dealer or mechanic directly, or you may have to pay for the work and ask the service contract company for reimbursement.

How long will I keep the car? Service contracts are not transferable from car to car, but sometimes can be transferred from owner to owner. If you don't plan to own the car for a long time, a long-term service contract may not be a practical purchase unless you can obtain value for it from the buyer of your car.

Where can I get service? What happens if I am traveling or

if I move? Under most service contracts, your car must normally be serviced by the selling dealership. In some contracts, you may use any mechanic you choose. Manufacturers have dealerships nationwide, and service may be available from any of their dealers. And most dealer contracts are part of a network that offers nationwide service, so you may be able to get service if you travel or move. Other companies give you service only in a specific geographical area.

How much does the service contract cost? While manufacturers service contracts generally offer the same coverage for all their new cars, the price changes by car model. Independent company and dealer service contracts base contract price on car make, model, condition (new or used), what is covered, and length of contract. Any dealer may offer more than one type of contract. You may be able to choose your coverage and cost.

What other costs will I have? After you pay for the contract, you may have other expenses. Service contracts, like insurance policies, have deductible amounts. Many contracts charge you for each unrelated repair. Some contracts charge you one fee per repair visit no matter how many repairs are made. Frequently, contracts limit the amount paid out for towing or rental car expenses, and you remain responsible for the costs of maintenance and repairs not covered. You may also have to pay cancellation or transfer fees if you sell your car or wish to end the contract.

Remember that service contracts can be purchased for both new and used vehicles.

11

Rip-offs: Beating the Huchsters at Their Own Game

New York Times, May 8, 1979

Undercover investigators for the Department of Transportation found in a survey of 62 automobile repair shops in seven cities that 53 cents of each service dollar was wasted on needless repairs . . .

The investigators, in the $66,000 study under the auspices of the University of Alabama, found that a customer stands only a 50-50 chance of getting his car repaired at the right price on any random visit.

Other surveys, including the one I recently did across the country, parallel those results. These disturbing numbers stand as mute witnesses to the dilemma faced by car owners seeking auto repairs.

THE GARAGE ATTENDANT COMETH—WITH AN ICE PICK

Ice picks are very versatile. When I was a kid, I marveled at the way the iceman performed magic on a huge block of ice—whittling, chipping, and carving out the exact size needed by his customer. All he ever used to accomplish his task was an ice pick.

Ask any air-conditioning ductwork installer what one of his most useful tools is, and no doubt he will reply, "an ice pick." They are just perfect for punching holes to start sheet-metal screws.

Put an ice pick in the hands of a good bartender and he or she can scalp a lemon without drawing a drop of juice, a prerequisite to the ideal lemon twist.

Put one in the hands of an unscrupulous service-station attendant and an ice pick becomes the perfect tire-punching tool.

Normal expenses on a driving vacation trip eat heavily into the bankroll, what with the current prices of gasoline, rooms, and meals. What you don't need are unnecessary expenses, the kind that some highway service-station attendants are more than willing to dole out.

A classic situation: you pull your out-of-state car into a service station and tell the man to fill it up and check the oil. While he is busy at your car, there is a mad rush for the rest rooms and refreshment machines as the whole family scatters helter-skelter. Upon your return to the car, the attendant greets you with a $25 tab for the gasoline and the bad news that one of your tires is leaking air.

You never noticed anything wrong on the road but, upon inspection, you find a leak. The tire is taken off the car and the attendant, after looking at its innards, says the puncture can be fixed, but the tire's safety is questionable. Concerned about your family, you agree to buy a new tire, thankful that the puncture was spotted and didn't develop into a blowout at high speed. A hundred dollars lighter, you pull away, feeling you did the right thing.

Unfortunately, you were just ripped off. An unattended car is a joy to behold, money in the bank for dishonest service-station workers. It takes only a second to puncture a tire with an ice pick or slash it with a pocket knife. A concealed screwdriver or wrench can be used to quickly loosen hoses, causing fluids to leak and giving the engine the appearance of a major disaster area. There are a number of other quick, easy and nefariously effective scare schemes a deft roadside magician can perform.

But there is a simple solution that will halt automobile molesters in their tracks. Don't leave the car. Stay with it until it has been gased and serviced. Get out of the car. Hound the attendant, track his every move. If he is honest, he shouldn't mind a bit. Always leave an adult guard with the car. Take turns at refreshing. If you are driving by yourself, have the car serviced first, then pull over to the side near the rest rooms, lock it, then refresh yourself.

Simple? You bet. But very effective. It could save you and yours many dollars and much anxiety—dollars that can be used for what they were saved for—vacationing—and anxiety that can be saved for when you get back to work.

So the next time you are on the road and you hear someone say, "The iceman cometh," make sure he doesn't have grease on his overalls.

—Bob Sikorsky
"Drive It Forever"
New York Times Syndication Sales Corp.

Not long after that column was published I received the following letter:

Dear Mr. Sikorsky,

Every time you or one of your colleagues cannot think of anything original, you start on the automobile mechanics. The electronic media do the same.

I do not deny that there are dishonest car mechanics. However, try this sometime: Go to a car dealership or a gas station and see what the mechanic drives. Then go to a hospital or a lawyer's office and see what the doctors and lawyers drive. Then maybe you will form a different opinion as to just who is really dishonest.

Sincerely, J.K.P.

I replied in part:

If you don't deny that there are dishonest mechanics, then what's the problem? Those are the ones I wrote about. I have no quarrel with competent, honest mechanics. They are a valuable asset to any community.

Your intimation that all doctors and lawyers who drive fancy cars must be dishonest is crazy. I wasn't aware that the kind of car a person drives is a reflection on his or her honesty.

RIP-OFF TIP-OFFS

It's easier to guard against fraud and dishonesty if one is aware of the methods used by cheats. Charging for work not done or repairs not needed, using old, used, or rebuilt parts when you are paying for new ones, repainting your old part and charging you for a new one are just some of the ways a dishonest operator will take your money.

But dishonesty can involve more than just the repair (or nonrepair) of your car. According to John Goodman, executive president of the California Automotive Service Councils, there are also oral or verbal abuses. These include such things as misleading advertising, bait and switch techniques, and scare tactics in selling practices. "We have little problem on reaching agreement on what is dishonest or what is an intent to deceive in the automotive repair field," says Goodman.

Here are some common rip-off techniques and favorite items a rip-off artist would just love to sell an unwary motorist: alternator, battery, tires, shock absorbers, coil springs, ball joints, fan belts, gas and oil additives, air and fuel filters, radiator caps, wiper blades, spark plugs and wires and other tune-up components.

"Add coil springs and load-leveling suspension parts to that list," says Marilyn Berton, of the Arizona attorney general's office. She notes that a lot of people are aware that shock absorbers are a favorite of part replacers, and rip-off artists, knowing this, are switching to coil springs and other suspension parts.

Most of these items are easily replaceable, turn a high profit, and don't take a lot of room to stock. Best way to know whether the shop has your wallet or best interests at heart is to have these parts checked and/or replaced before leaving home. That way you know they are in good condition, and it is highly unlikely they will go bad in a few thousand miles.

How many times have you heard someone say "Hey buddy, your rear axle is bad and needs replacing?" Not too many, I'll bet. And for good reason. It wouldn't be very practical to stock or replace them. Rear axles are one of the most durable parts on a car and rarely go bad. For these reasons you won't see this kind of part being sold by part changers or rip-offs.

But the above list of parts are easy to stock (many times, one kind fits all), easy to replace (while you are having lunch or breakfast new shocks or coil springs can be put on your car) and profitable. That's not saying that some, if not all, of these items won't have to be replaced periodically. For they will. Just be on guard against anyone trying to sell you a new part before the old one's time is up.

Other rip-off techniques involve outright sabotage of the car. Cutting fan belts, puncturing tires, spraying oil on shock absorbers to make it appear they are leaking, pointing out air-conditioner condensation—this is normal—underneath the car and saying it is some important fluid leaking, or the old scam of checking your oil or transmission fluid and not pushing the dip stick fully in so that it appears a quart or more low (short sticking). The attendant then puts a pour spout in an empty can and pretends to add the missing fluid. You of course get charged for the full quart.

If your car doesn't normally use oil, chances are it isn't going to start all at once. Best way to guard against this kind of thievery is to get out of the car and double check the oil or fluids yourself.

Someone may tell you that your radiator is very hot or your oil filter is overheating. Unless you notice a rise in the engine temperature gauge, ignore these two ploys. Both of these items are supposed to be hot.

Do you know what a rumble strip is? No, it's not a street in New York city but a series of raised impressions on a road surface that warn drivers if they are going off the road or approaching the end of a highway or toll booth. Some states place sections of rumble strips at random intervals to alert drowsy freeway drivers.

Some uninformed motorists, when they hit these strips and hear the loud noise, think that something is wrong and head for the nearest service station. I've heard some hairy stories about the number of new tires sold to rumble strip novices.

Here's a good rule of thumb: if you didn't notice anything wrong with the car prior to pulling into a service station—let's say you are stopping to get gas—chances are nothing is wrong with the car. It's unlikely that something will go bad while you are gasing up. It pays to be keen and cautious when pulling into strange service stations or repair shops. And as we saw from my column above, never leave your car unoccupied when stopping for service.

In a number of stops I made where I deliberately left the mechanic alone, I was ripped off or the car was sabotaged. It's more difficult for someone to disable the car or fake a repair when you or someone else is standing there watching.

Always accompany a mechanic when he offers to take the vehicle for a test drive. You will be better able to describe the symptoms and at the same time keep an eye on him—just in case.

My wife took the car into a Las Vegas, Nevada repair shop and was greeted by two mechanics. After listening to her describe the problem, and before she could object, one of them jumped in the car and sped off. When he returned he told her the car had "transmission problems, lady."

After hearing this, the second mechanic, over my wife's objections, got into the car and took off on another test drive. At this point, even though she knew I was nearby observing, she began to panic. The mechanics, working in pairs, had intimidated her to the point where she felt the situation was out-of-hand.

When the second driver returned after a lengthy absence, he disagreed with the first diagnosis and insisted she needed a complete tune-up—and that the time to have it was NOW. He emphasized that it was very dangerous to drive the car in its present condition as severe damage could be done to the engine. And he wasn't kidding! For when she shook loose of the two clowns by telling them she had to go to the bank to get some money, I immediately noticed that the engine temperature had skyrocketed. During one of the test drives, the electric fan just happened to go bad.

Bolster your defense against rip-offs by getting to know your car. If you know it is in good shape—remember, have it checked over thoroughly before starting out on a trip—and someone later suggests a questionable repair, you can be almost certain that they are trying to sell you something you don't need.

Always keep in mind; however, that it is possible for any part to go bad at any time, and for that reason you should listen to a mechanic when he suggests a repair. It will be up to you to decide whether it is legitimate. If he mentions one of the items we have just listed, your guard should go up, but you shouldn't discount his warning. If doubt persists, get a second opinion.

MORE RIP-OFF TIP-OFFS

Dear Bob:

I am a widow and 66 years old. I took my car to a service station because it was stalling on me—they told me it needed a tune-up. I made an appointment, and a friend went along with me in her car. We left my car, and they said it would be ready in two hours. When we returned to pick it up, they said they didn't have time to do it so they sent the car to another of their service stations located on the freeway. They were to call me later.

Well at 8 o'clock that evening they called and said they had the refrigeration unit tore apart, and as you can see from the copy of the enclosed invoice, everything they did. I had to get a lawyer to get my car—plus it still didn't run, it would still stall on me. I took it to a dealer and all that was wrong with the car was that it needed a new computer card.

I am writing this for all people young and old to watch out for rip-off places like this.

Thank you,
Mrs. J. J. R.

Someone might try to get you to sign a blank work order or authorization form or forget to give you your copy. If a mechanic refuses to give you a written estimate or won't fill out a work order, or is vague and hems and haws about the price of parts and labor, or insists on a cash-only deal (see chapter 10 on the benefits of using a credit card to pay for auto repairs) take your business elsewhere. The above lady signed the work order for a tune-up but forgot to get her copy. You can see what happened. Here are some other tip-offs where a rip-off might show his hand.

The person who seems overly vague about what is wrong with your car or what could be involved in the repair, giving you a long list of what it could be but avoiding specifics is a beware sign. It's likely he is trying to leave the door open for himself when he "gets into" the vehicle. Although some problems can't be found until, say, the engine is torn down, they are usually rare. Most mechanical problems can be diagnosed without a major teardown.

Never trust a mechanic who offers a diagnosis by just listening to your description and who doesn't bother to look at the car. More likely than not, he's just guessing. These Johnny-on-the-spot "expert" opinions—I know what's wrong for I've heard this many times before—aren't the hallmark of a quality repair technician or facility.

Be suspicious of the we-can-do-it-right-now guys like the Las Vegas duo that cornered my wife. Like her, don't make hasty decisions. Don't be pressured into something you feel uncomfortable about. Take your time, it's your money and your car. Be certain before you give the go ahead. Remember, there usually is good reason for overeagerness: they want your money now—before you have time to think about it, change your mind, or leave.

Newspaper advertised specials that seem too good to be true usually are! Some of these are bait advertising, worded to lure you into the shop for a low-cost oil change or free safety inspection. Once there, it's likely other work will be suggested. Although many "specials" are legitimate, scouring the papers for a good deal could cost you in the long run. There is no substitute for a solid relationship with an honest competent garage. You are better off paying a few extra dollars in a shop where your car and face are known than running all over town trying to save a couple of bucks on a oil change here or a tune-up there.

Coupon books also fall into that category. These money-saving booklets might be just the ticket to get you to bring your car back to the same shop time and time again. On each visit an attempt will probably be made to sell you other parts and services, in addition to the coupon special, which you might or might not need.

A friend of mine took his car to a national chain repair outlet that was running a too-good-to-be-true oil change and lube special along with a free safety inspection. He did get the "special" but then was told he needed new brakes and front-end struts, which he wisely did not buy.

A few months later at the same shop, again for a special oil change and lube with a safety inspection, he was told he needed new coil springs. No one even mentioned his struts and front brakes, which only two months earlier were proclaimed bad. Seems like coil springs were the promotional item that month.

Watch out for scare tactics. An admonition like "I wouldn't drive this car another mile, lady,"—especially after you have just come 2,000 miles without a hint of trouble—or "Oh, this type of engine always gives us a lot of trouble," should be viewed with healthy suspicion. Negative head shaking, wiping of the brow, or statements or tactics meant to scare are things to watch and listen for. Don't let someone plant a seed of doubt in your mind for it can grow and blossom into a costly paper tiger. If you have doubts or feel threatened, just leave.

A woman in an Omaha repair shop told me about the time she and her late husband were vacationing in California and about to cross a long stretch of desert. A service station attendant told her husband that the tires were bad. After leaving, he became frightened that something might happen in the desert ahead, turned around, and backtracked some 40 odd miles to the station. Over his wife's protests, he bought a new set of tires even though the ones on the car were practically new. Maybe some of those *Mechanic On Duty* signs so common at service stations and repair shops across the country should be prefaced by another word: *WARNING*.

Don't underestimate what a seed of doubt or fear, properly planted by an expert rip-off, can do. Many years ago my two aunts and a friend came west on vacation. A service station convinced them that they needed new shock absorbers although the car was brand new with only 2,600 miles on the odometer. When I later found out that they had been had, I took the car back to the station and demanded the old shocks be put back on and the money refunded. Under threats of being reported—which I did anyway—the station happened to find the old shocks on a backroom shelf, replaced them and refunded the money. But, the attendant had so well convinced my aunts that the original shocks were bad that they worried all the way back to Pennsylvania.

I talked to an editor at a popular woman's magazine and she stated that her readers were too savvy to fall for any of these lines. "Don't be too sure," I countered. "There are an awful lot of smart people running around with lightened purses and wallets."

If your car is less than five years old or has less than 50,000 miles on it, don't buy any parts for the emissions control system. Each one, including the expensive catalytic converter, is covered by a government mandated warranty and must be replaced free by the manufacturer if found defective. Some shops won't tell you about this law and will charge you for parts and labor you could get gratis. This warranty applies even though you purchased the car from a previous owner.

OUT-OF-STATE PLATES: LICENSES FOR LICENSE?

Out-of-state plates signal the dishonest service dealer that a car is ripe for a rip-off. The occupants are away from home, heading toward a destination with some kind of time schedule to meet. They aren't familiar with local customs and practices. They are vulnerable. They will, as a rule, do most anything to keep the car on the road. In other words, they are sitting ducks. And Lordy, do some operators take advantage of that.

Watch for license plate scanners. Look for the attendant who seeks out a spot where he can inconspicuously glance at your plates. If you see one doing it, be on guard. Expect something to happen. Expect them to say that you need tires, shocks-coil springs, or something. And be happy you know where to tell them to go.

Many shops, especially interstate service stations, might not be after big-ticket items. They are satisfied with smaller 15- or 20-dollar takes. And for good reason. Run enough of these through the cash register, and you have a tidy profit at the end of the day.

It's a lot safer too. It's rare that anyone comes back. Even if a driver later suspects that he was taken, he isn't going to return to make a ruckus over a $15 fuel filter. Main items involved here: fuel and air filters, radiator caps, oil and gasoline additives.

If you must leave your car at a shop be certain that all valuables are either removed or locked in the trunk and that you take the trunk key with you. I lost a good shirt that caught a mechanic's eye somewhere between Chicago and Omaha.

MECHANICAL DRIFTERS

"Commission pay is a damnation, it's a curse," says Ron Weiner, president of the National Institute for Automotive Service Excellence (ASE). Weiner says paying mechanics on a commission basis is a throwback to the depression days when a guy came into a shop looking for work. The owner told him to toss his tools in the corner, and they would split whatever he made. The practice has endured—albeit in somewhat modified form—to the present, and predominates throughout the industry.

If a shop hires an honest man there's no problem, says Weiner. But if an opportunist is hired, all he might care about is getting the work out fast and making as much money as he can. This in turn invariably leads to cheating, overcharges, and unnecessary work.

Marilyn Berton calls these commission-pay boys "50-percenters," mechanical drifters who, even after an undercover operation has exposed them, will find work in another shop in another town. Like bad pennies, they always seem to turn up.

Too few of us make use of our intuition. If you don't feel right about a shop or if you only suspect you might be getting ripped off—stop it before it goes any further. Listen to your intuition. More likely than not, it's right.

In a Kansas City repair shop waiting room, I asked one of two women if it was a good, honest shop. She shrugged her shoulders and summed up the predicament of many car owners when she replied, "I certainly hope so." I couldn't help but notice her fingers were crossed as she spoke.

It's funny, but some consumers have a curious way of reacting to being ripped-off. Those who have been taken attain folklore status among friends and relatives. Their stories are told with reverence and glee. Like the time Old Uncle Walter got ripped in that New Mexico desert town back in '55. No doubt you know someone, perhaps yourself, who has been badly ripped-off. Hopefully, this book will help put an end to modern day rip-off tales.

Although there's growing concern and action being taken to stem dishonest repair practices across the country, the consumer still must be on guard. For in the final analysis, it comes down to just you and the shop; and the only thing that separates you from getting ripped off or receiving an honest repair is knowledge of your car and knowing what to look for or avoid at a repair facility.

AUTOMATIC TRANSMISSIONS: FERTILE GROUND FOR RIP-OFFS

Your car is running smoothly, but before using it for your upcoming vacation, you decide to get the automatic transmission checked. You cannot resist the ad you saw for a low-priced transmission tune-up.

The next thing you know, your car's transmission is spread all over a workbench, and you are told it will cost $800 to have the transmission repaired. You are at a loss because now you cannot drive the car to comparison shop for repair costs . . . or find out if the car actually had a transmission problem. Reluctantly, you keep your car where it is and pay their price.

—"Automatic Transmission Repair"
Federal Trade Commission in cooperation
with the Automotive Parts Rebuilders Association and
the Automatic Transmission Rebuilders Association

Perhaps no other single mechanical unit on a car is more susceptible to rip-off schemes than is the automatic transmission. There are a number of reasons for this. The automatic transmission is, in most cases, a marvel of efficiency and durability, working flawlessly for tens of thousands of miles. It requires very little attention and therefore, has the distinction of being one of the car's most-ignored mechanical units.

Automatic transmissions are mysterious and complicated even for many learned mechanics and technicians. Clutches, gears, seals, and passages galore, the insides of an automatic looks like the leftovers from a Star Wars mechanical rehearsal. Little wonder the average person knows naught about it.

When a car owner finally decides to service the transmission, either because it doesn't work like it used to or is losing fluid to the garage driveway, he or she usually ends up taking it to one of the transmission specialty shops. And you can almost bet your boots it's one of those advertising a low-cost $4.95 transmission service special, (Fig. 11-1).

What is an automatic transmission service? A normal transmission service and inspection will usually include all or most of the following: test drive vehicle, check transmission fluid level and condition, check and/or adjust manual linkage, remove transmission pan, adjust bands, clean screen or replace filter, add fresh fluid as required, install new pan gasket, and replace the pan (Fig. 11-2).

Fig. 11-1. Advertisements like this one are usually a ploy to persuade you to have other repairs done.

Fig. 11-2. A mechanic might bring the transmission pan to you for inspection.

If the shop is unscrupulous, they might bring the transmission pan to you and cite the many fine metal particles in it as evidence of the transmission wearing out. Customers have fallen for this scam because it does look like something is wearing. And something is wearing, but the wear in this case is usually normal. Those fine metal particles are nothing but normal wear debris that has accumulated in the pan. Most of it was generated as the car broke-in during the first 2,000 miles of driving. Unless there are chunks of metal or parts laying in the pan, fine wear debris is no cause for alarm.

If your transmission was working fine when you took it in for servicing, chances are there is nothing wrong with it, so don't be influenced by the wear particle or any other ploy. If a shop recommends the transmission be torn down to find a problem, get in writing why the teardown is necessary and what the maximum cost of the repair will be. In cases like this, before any teardown is authorized you should obtain a second opinion.

According to the Michigan Bureau of Automotive Regulation, "A good transmission mechanic, in most cases, can diagnose whether a problem is internal or external without removing the transmission from your vehicle. Sometimes when there is an external problem, it can be easily and quickly fixed without teardowns and overhaul."

Once you authorize a teardown, however, you are committed. Even though you might decide not to go ahead with the suggested repair that the teardown found, you will still have to pay the shop to put the transmission back together and sometimes that can be quite expensive. Any estimate to diagnose transmission problems should specify the cost to reassemble in the event repairs are decided against.

SHIFTY OPERATORS

Not long before I drove through Michigan surveying repair shops, the attorney general and secretary of state offices had recently concluded *Operation Shifty*, a three-month undercover investigation of transmission repair shops. A number of shops were closed and charged with performing unnecessary work. Arrests were made, and the entire undercover operation was the focus of statewide publicity.

Fred Pirochta, director of Michigan Repair Facility Division and man in charge of the operation says, "There is no question that because of the amount of publicity Operation Shifty received, public awareness is at a high. The problem, however, is not only with Michigan, but with every state in the Union."

The residual effect of the publicity received by Operation Shifty was, Pirochta believes, no doubt responsible for a curious anomaly I encountered while visiting a variety of repair shops in the Detroit area: each one I stopped at diagnosed and fixed my problem quickly, and not one of them charged me!

One of the methods used by the automatic transmission repair shops targeted by Operation Shifty, was to tell the customer that the transmission had to be disassembled for a modest price before it could be checked out. Invariably, said Pirochta, once the transmission was apart, the customers got the bad news that it would cost hundreds of dollars to replace or repair it. The customer, feeling trapped, usually gave the go-ahead.

In the wake of Operation Shifty, a number of mechanics came forth and described their modus operandi. What they had to say can help you the next time you take your car into any repair shop: customers were sized up when they drove in. Prime targets? Owners of newer cars. Why? Because they had more money invested in the car and were more likely to be willing to spend some money to protect their investment.

The automatic transmission is one of the most expensive yet durable components on a car. Rarely, if they are serviced as per manufacturer's recommendations, will they ever need repair. Don't be sucked into a free inspection just because it's free. "If it ain't broke, don't fix it."

INCOMPETENCY: THE REAL
BANE OF THE REPAIR INDUSTRY

Although the perceived differences between dishonest and incompetent mechanics are as distinct as night and day, their bottom lines can be very similar: the customer pays for something he or she doesn't need. Incompetent mechanics can be the most honest people in the world—they don't mean to do any harm, but they do. Incompetence is a two-edged sword, and both sides of the blade are sharp. An incompetent is likely to bungle a repair, and you end up taking the car elsewhere to have it fixed right. And the bungled work, in turn, is likely to cause other problems, problem you didn't have when you pulled into the shop but which were created by the incompetent mechanic.

A lot of present day incompetence can be traced to the fact that many mechanics are intimidated by newer high-tech and computer-controlled cars. They assume any problem has to be complicated and forget to go back to basics. Many rely on equipment they are only marginally familiar with or that is outdated. The equipment itself can be incompetent, misleading even a good mechanic and making the customer pay for unnecessary repairs. Even good equipment can hinder more than help if the mechanics don't have proper training to run it.

"Incompetence," says ASC's Goodman, "is far too prevalent in our industry." He suggests that when you find a bad operator, spread the word. When you find a good one, do the same.

INCONVENIENCE AND LOST TIME:
NO COMPENSATION FOR THEM

In "Anatomy of a Complaint," a report he wrote for the California BAR when he was deputy chief, Goodman says,

> There is nothing in the (new car) warranty which compensates for the inconvenience of being without one's car or for car rental allowance or for missed business appointments or for extra motel bills or taxi fares or for telephone calls. In terms of emotional disturbance, the inconvenience of warranty repairs on a new car rates near the top of the scale.
>
> Inconvenience to the customer by making him wait is a plague that each industry or organization would like to shed. In the race to see who can irritate the customer most by not being

on time, the automotive repair gang wins it all. Whoever is in second place is so distant that it is not a contest at all.

The aggravation grows because alternatives are automatically removed. If the service is too slow in a restaurant, we can get up and leave. If the service station attendant is hard to find, we need not wait; we can drive on to the next station. But once our car is dismantled, our power to control the schedule or speed up the work consists solely of voicing our emotions. And voice it they do. This complaint is usually on top of all the others.

Inconvenience and time lost pursuing any shoddy repair or rip-off aren't customer compensated. Add the time spent chasing a matter through arbitration panels, contacting private or government consumer groups or attorneys, or time logged in the courts and you get some idea of just how frustrating and time-consuming the wake of shoddy or rip-off repairs can be. You might eventually recover your money or get your car fixed right, but the time you spent doing it is lost. And when you look at it, that time could be the most precious thing of all.

When the consideration of time and inconvenience are introduced into the repair equation, competent repair—doing it right the first time at a fair price—preventive maintenance, and knowledge of your car loom ever more portentous.

12

The Fine Art of Effective Complaining

The people who really get victimized are those who don't fight back; those who want to believe and trust are the ones who really get picked.

—Fred Pirochta,
Director of the Repair Facility Division of Michigan
Bureau of Automotive Regulation

Next to mail-order problems, consumer dissatisfaction with auto repair practices is the most frequent complaint fielded by consumer protection agencies in the United States. It far outranks the next in line.

To this point we have covered important aspects of having your car repaired. Ideally, the book should end here. But in this imperfect world, no matter how hard we try, our best efforts can sometimes run afoul. What do we do if we find the repair unsatisfactory, or unauthorized work was done, or you feel you have been ripped off? If you've followed the advice given here so far, chances are that won't happen. But if it does, here's what to do.

RETURNING TO THE SHOP TO COMPLAIN

The very first thing to do is take the car and the work order back to the repair shop. Don't be too fast to condemn and keep in mind that even the best and most honest operator can make mistakes.

Explain in detail why you are unhappy with the repair. If the problem is visible, point it out. If the problem only surfaces when the car is moving, insist that a mechanic drive the car with you. The more you can show and tell, the better.

Many times customer dissatisfaction can be traced to a simple misunderstanding between the shop and the car owner and honest dialog between the two will often resolve the problem. Always take the car back to the shop that did the work and do your best to resolve your complaint. If the shop is at fault, it should be willing to rectify the situation. A good shop doesn't need or want any more hassle than you do.

When you talk to the shop's owner, manager, or mechanic, take the Michigan Department of State, Bureau of Automotive Regulation's advice:

1. Know your basic rights.

2. Be courteous and calm.

3. Explain the problem accurately and state what you think would be a fair settlement.

4. If you are willing to negotiate, say so; in many disputes neither side is 100% right.

5. If your attempt to settle your problem with the facility fails, you may file a formal complaint . . . You may wish to advise the facility that you intend to file a complaint.

Consumer's rights vary from state to state. It is important that you know your rights prior to instituting any type of complaint action against a repair facility. For instance, under Michigan law, where most shops doing motor vehicle repair are registered and regulated by the Michigan Department of State, a customer has the following rights:

1. The facility must give you a written estimate before any repairs that will cost $20 or more. On repairs costing under $20, you are entitled to a written estimate if you request one.

2. The facility must contact you and get your permission before doing any work that will exceed the written estimate by more than $10 or 10% (whichever is less).

3. When repairs are completed, you are entitled to a detailed written invoice (final bill) describing all the work done and the money charged.

4. Unless you tell the facility to dispose of them, you have a right to receive and inspect the parts that were replaced in the repair of your vehicle.

5. If the facility has violated the Motor Vehicle Service and Repair Act in servicing your vehicle, they cannot take legal action to collect money you owe them or to enforce a lien on your vehicle.

Do not take the car to another shop to have it repaired. That will only add coals to the fire and will seriously dim your chances of having the first shop fix it properly in the event they were at fault.

But if you can't come to terms with the repair facility you must take matters into your own hands. As the Michigan advisory mentions, your next action should be filing some kind of formal complaint. Let's look at some of the most effective kinds.

THE BETTER BUSINESS BUREAU

Many of us live within driving distance of a Better Business Bureau (BBB) office. Even if you don't, there's probably an office listed in your phone book. No need to go in person because a complaint can be initiated by phone.

After you have registered your complaint in as much detail as possible, the BBB will send a letter to the repair shop advising them of the complaint. BBB personnel tell me that many settlements are reached at this early stage. In other cases, additional mediation by the BBB or even formal arbitration might be needed to resolve the complaint.

In addition to this straightforward complaint process, over 25,000 companies nationwide have voluntarily signed up to be included in a BBB arbitration process. Dealerships, independent repair shops and automotive chain stores are among the many that participate. If your complaint happens to be against one of the participating companies then any arbitrated settlement—except those pursued through the Auto Line program described below—is binding on both the consumer and the company.

WARRANTY WORK

If your car is still under warranty and the work in question was done by a dealership's service department, you should first take the car back to the dealer just as you would do with any other shop. If you receive no satisfaction then complain to the manufacturer's regional office. The number and address and the outlined complaint procedure are in your owner's manual. If that doesn't bring results there are a number of other avenues of action.

AUTO LINE

Contact the BBB's Auto Line program. This special consumer service attempts to settle disputes through mediation and arbitration involving the manufacturer's of many domestic and foreign automobiles (call the local BBB office to see if your car is one of them).

After hearing both sides of the story—you will have to be present at the BBB's office—the arbitrator, a specially trained individual selected from the community, rends a decision which is binding on the manufacturer in most cases. The consumer is free to either accept or reject it. It's a no-lose proposition for the consumer with a new car complaint.

Dean Determan, vice president of the Council of Better Business Bureaus, says over 30,000 cases are arbitrated through the Auto Line program each year resulting in a 78% consumer acceptance of decisions. In addition, over 4,000 cars were bought back by the manufacturers because of the arbitrator's ruling.

Although the Auto Line program, at this writing, involves all GM vehicles, and a number of imports, other major manufacturers don't subscribe to it. Some have their own procedures. For instance, Ford and Chrysler have in-house arbitration processes. Again, check your owner's manual for details because the procedure varies from manufacturer to manufacturer.

AUTOCAP: THE AUTOMOTIVE CONSUMER ACTION PROGRAM

Another source of consumer help is the AUTOCAP program. AUTOCAP is an informal third-party mediation system designed to improve dealer/customer relations by providing review and mediation of automotive disputes involving participating franchised new car and truck dealers.

According to the *Automotive Customer Relations Directory*, a manual distributed by the Consumers Affairs Division of the National Automobile Dealers Association (NADA), AUTOCAP works to resolve disputes in two ways. First, AUTOCAP staff will attempt to settle the dispute through informal mediation between the parties. Unresolved disputes are mediated by an impartial panel consisting of consumer representatives and auto dealers; a minimum of 50 percent must be consumer representatives. The panel recommends a solution based on the facts of the case. A majority of cases mediated by AUTOCAP are successfully resolved at the staff level; few (only 14 percent in 1987) require review by the consumer/dealer panel.

AUTOCAP is most effective at mediating disputes involving participating new car dealers. However, several auto manufacturers/importers have agreed to participate in AUTOCAP, in accordance with the National AUTOCAP Standards, to assist in resolving their customers' warranty and product-reliability disputes. These companies are Alfa Romeo, Austin Rover (Sterling), BMW, Fiat, Honda, Isuzu, Jaguar, Mazda, Mitsubishi, Nissan, Peugeot, Rolls Royce, Saab-Scania, Volvo, and Yugo. (These companies can also support or participate in alternative dispute resolution programs, such as state "lemon law" programs.)

Several state and local dealer associations currently sponsor AUTOCAP. Some programs mediate only disputes between franchised new car dealers and consumers. Other programs mediate new car warranty and product reliability disputes involving participating manufacturers, as well as dealer/consumer disputes. Unless a particular state or local program has obtained appropriate commitments from participating manufacturers and or dealers, the decision to accept or reject an AUTOCAP recommendation is purely voluntary and at the sole discretion of the participating manufacturer or dealer. In all cases, panel recommendations are nonbinding on consumers. Sponsoring associations should be contacted for details on a particular state or local program.

To assist those of you who wish to employ the AUTOCAP process, here are the current locations of sponsoring AUTOCAP associations:

Arizona

ARIZONA AUTOMOBILE DEALERS ASSOCIATION
Keith Andresen, Executive Vice President
Jean Fankhauser, AUTOCAP Administrator
P.O. Box 5438
Phoenix, AZ 85010
(602) 252-2386

California

MOTOR CAR DEALERS ASSOCIATION
  OF SOUTHERN CALIFORNIA
Scott Thomas Wilk, Asst. Executive
  Vice President
Bruce Sedlezky, AUTOCAP Manager
5757 W. Century Boulevard
Suite 310
Los Angeles, CA 90045
(1-800) 262-1492 (toll free, California only)
(213) 642-7744
(Southern California only)

MOTOR CAR DEALERS ASSOCIATION
  OF SAN DIEGO COUNTY
Robert T. Coleman, Executive Vice President
Lupe Lutich, AUTOCAP Manager
2525 Camino Del Rio South
Suite 103
San Diego, CA 92108
(619) 296-2265
(San Diego County only)

Colorado

METROPOLITAN DENVER AUTOMOBILE
  DEALERS ASSOCIATION
William D. Barrow, President
Mary Elizabeth Plum, AUTOCAP Contact
517 E. 16th Avenue
Denver, CO 80203
(303) 831-1722

Connecticut

CONNECTICUT AUTOMOTIVE TRADES
   ASSOCIATION, INC.
Stephen Gabriel, Executive Vice President
Dwight Burnham, AUTOCAP Manager
91 Elm Street
Hartford, CT 06106
(203) 293-2500

District of Columbia

AUTOMOTIVE TRADE ASSOCIATION OF
   THE NATIONAL CAPITAL AREA
Gerard N. Murphy, President
Joanne Ford, Senior Consumer Advisor
Christopher Neuber, Consumer Advisor
15873 Crabbs Branch Way
Rockville, MD 20855
(301) 670-1110
(Washington, D.C., Northern Virginia,
Montgomery & Prince Georges Counties,
Maryland, only)

Florida

BETTER BUSINESS BUREAU OF N.E. FLORIDA, INC.
George J. Hood, Director
3100 University Boulevard, S.
Suite 239
Jacksonville, FL 32216
(904) 721-2339
(Duval County only)

SOUTH FLORIDA AUTOMOBILE AND TRUCK
   DEALERS ASSOCIATION
Richard A. Baker, Executive Vice President
Francine Attal, AUTOCAP Coordinator
BBB of S. Florida, Inc.16291 N.W. 57th Avenue
Miami, FL 33014-6709
(305) 624-1828 (Dade & Monroe Counties)
(305) 522-2886 (Broward County)

Cathie Roth Rockwood, AUTOCAP Consultant
BBB of Palm Beach, Martin & St. Lucie
3015 Exchange Court
West Palm Beach, FL 33409
(305) 686-6168 (Palm Beach)
(305) 272-4445 (Boca Raton & Delray)

Georgia

GEORGIA AUTOMOBILE DEALERS ASSOCIATION
William F. Morie, President
Frank Carlson, AUTOCAP Director
4000 Cumberland Parkway
Building 900, Suite A
Atlanta, GA 30339
(404) 432-1658

Hawaii

HAWAII AUTOMOBILE DEALERS ASSOCIATION
Hardy Hutchinson, Manager
Pioneer Plaza, Suite 1777
900 Fort Street Mall
Honolulu, HI 96813
(808) 526-0159

Illinois

ILLINOIS NEW CAR & TRUCK
   DEALERS ASSOCIATION
Peter Sander, President
Mark Harting, AUTOCAP Staff Coordinator
P.O. Box 3045
Springfield, IL 62708
(217) 753-4513

Kentucky

KENTUCKY AUTOMOBILE DEALERS ASSOCIATION
Robert Newberry, Executive Vice President
Jane Clark, AUTOCAP Director

Independent Arbitration Services, Inc.
Lane Allen Plaza
845 Lane Allen Road
Lexington, KY 40504
(606) 277-0511

Maine

MAINE AUTOMOBILE DEALERS ASSOCIATION, INC.
Thomas Brown, Executive Vice President
P.O. Box 2667
Augusta, ME 04330
(207) 623-3882

Maryland

See District of Columbia

Michigan

MICHIGAN AUTOMOBILE DEALERS ASSOCIATION
A. Barry McGuire, Executive Vice President
Dennis Schwartz, AUTOCAP Director
P.O. Box 2525
East Lansing, MI 48823
(1-800) 292-1923 (toll free, Michigan only)
(517) 351-7800
(Does not serve Macomb, Oakland or
   Wayne Counties)

Montana

MONTANA AUTOMOBILE DEALERS ASSOCIATION
Dean Mansfield, Executive Vice President
Kevin Mazzucola, AUTOCAP Director
501 N. Sanders
Helena, MT 59601
(406) 442-1233

New Hampshire

New Hampshire Automobile Dealers
  Association
Daniel McLeod, President
Richard L. Rodman, AUTOCAP Director
P.O. Box 2337
Concord, NH 03302-2337
(603) 224-2369

New Mexico

New Mexico Automotive Dealers
  Association
Raymond Berube, Jr., Executive Vice
  President
Greg Scipes, AUTOCAP Director
3815 Hawkins, N.E.
Albuquerque, NM 87109
(505) 345-1221

New York

Broome County Automobile Dealers
  Council, Inc.
Louis Gennett, Manager, Special Programs
P.O. Box 995
Binghamton, NY 13902
(607) 723-7127
(Broome County only)

Capital District Automobile
  Dealers Association
Daniel P. Harrison, Executive Director
1237 Central Avenue
Albany, NY 12205
(518) 438-0584
(Albany, Saratoga, Schenectady &
  Troy Counties)

GREATER NEW YORK AUTOMOBILE DEALERS
   ASSOCIATION, INC.
Mark Schienberg, Executive Vice President
Mindy L. Martin, AUTOCAP Manager
18-10 Whitestone Parkway
Whitestone, NY 11357
(1-800) 245-4640 (toll free, New York only)
(718) 746-5900
(NYC, LI and Westchester County only)

NIAGARA FRONTIER AUTOMOBILE DEALERS
   ASSOCIATION
Richard K. Welte, President
Sharon Telis, AUTOCAP Director
1144 Wehrle Drive
Williamsville, NY 14221
(716) 631-8510
(Erie County only)

ROCHESTER AUTOMOBILE DEALERS ASSOCIATION
Donald N. Stahl, Executive Director
Nancy Magill, AUTOCAP Manager
179 Lake Avenue
Rochester, NY 14608
(716) 458-7150

NEW YORK STATE AUTOMOBILE
   DEALERS ASSOCIATION
Norma Sharp, Executive Vice President
Diane Bowen, AUTOCAP Manager
37 Elk Street, Box 7347
Albany, NY 12224
(1-800) 342-9208 (toll free, New York only)
(518) 463-1148
(Serves balance of state)

North Carolina

NORTH CAROLINA AUTOMOBILE DEALERS
   ASSOCIATION
B. Wade Isaacs, Executive Vice President

Diane Turner, AUTOCAP Director
Sally Gregg, AUTOCAP Manager
P.O. Box 12167
Raleigh, NC 27605-2167
(919) 828-4421

North Dakota

AUTOMOBILE DEALERS ASSOCIATION
   OF NORTH DAKOTA
Robert L. Lamp, Executive Vice President
Carmelle Schulte, AUTOCAP Manager
P.O. Box 2524
Fargo, ND 58108
(701) 293-6822

Ohio

CLEVELAND AUTOMOBILE DEALERS ASSOCIATION
Gary S. Adams, Executive Vice President
1367 E. 6th Street
Suite 300
Cleveland, OH 44114
(216) 241-2880
(Metropolitan Cleveland only)

OHIO AUTOMOBILE DEALERS ASSOCIATION
Tim Doran, Executive Vice President
Frank Caltrider, AUTOCAP Manager
1366 Dublin Road
Columbus, OH 43215
(614) 487-9000
(Serves balance of state)

Oklahoma

TULSA AUTOMOBILE DEALERS ASSOCIATION
Thomas Marsh, Executive Secretary
808 Oneok Building
100 W. 5th Street
Tulsa, OK 74103
(918) 587-0141
(Metropolitan Tulsa only)

Oregon

OREGON AUTOMOBILE DEALERS ASSOCIATION
Wallace Peters, Executive Vice President
Norm Foster, AUTOCAP Manager
P.O. Box 14460
Portland, OR 97214
(503) 233-5044

South Carolina

SOUTH CAROLINA AUTOMOBILE & TRUCK
  DEALERS ASSOCIATION
Patrick Watson, Executive Vice President
Peggy Stork, AUTOCAP Director
1517 Laurel Street
Columbia, SC 29201
(803) 254-4040

South Dakota

SOUTH DAKOTA AUTOMOBILE DEALERS
  ASSOCIATION
R. Van Johnson, Executive Vice President
David Larson, AUTOCAP Manager
P.O. Box 80540
Sioux Falls, SD 57116
(605) 336-2616

Texas

TEXAS AUTOMOBILE DEALERS ASSOCIATION
Gene Fondren, Executive Vice President
Terry Williams, AUTOCAP Manager
P.O. Box 1028
Austin, TX 78767
(512) 476-2686

Vermont

VERMONT AUTOMOBILE DEALERS ASSOCIATION
Marilyn Miller, Executive Director

P.O. Box 561
Montpelier, VT 05602
(1-800) 642-5149 (toll free, Vermont only)
(802) 223-6635

Virginia

Northern Virginia: See District of Columbia

VIRGINIA AUTOMOBILE DEALERS ASSOCIATION
J. Ronald Nowland, Executive Vice
   President
Ronald Croy, AUTOCAP Director
P.O. Box 5407
Richmond, VA 23220
(804) 359-3578
(Serves balance of state)

Washington

PUGET SOUND AUTOMOBILE DEALERS ASSOCIA-
TION
James Hammond, Executive Vice President
Shannon Gilmore, AUTOCAP Coordinator
16101 Greenwood Avenue N.
Building 9900
Seattle, WA 98133
(206) 623-2034

Wisconsin

WISCONSIN AUTOMOBILE & TRUCK DEALERS
   ASSOCIATION
Gary Williams, President
David Williams, Vice President
Linda Poulsen, AUTOCAP Manager
P.O. Box 5345
Madison, WI 53705
(608) 251-3023

When any type of arbitration is undertaken to resolve a complaint, it's always a good idea to determine beforehand which parties
are bound by the arbitrator's decision.

STILL MORE WAYS TO GET HELP

You can file a complaint in small claims court or contact one of the local media action or consumer hot line services (some, such as Call For Action serve consumers nationally). Many newspapers have consumer complaint or ombudsman columns that attempt to settle consumer disputes. And you can always consult a private attorney.

If the shop in question displays some type of certification or group affiliation logo, or if your car was serviced at a national chain store or oil company service station, first complain in writing to their home offices. Then I suggest you take one of the many other avenues of action described in this section. If it is an AAA approved shop, and you are a member of AAA, you should first complain to AAA (see chapter 7).

Go to or phone a local or state consumer protection office. They are familiar with local businesses and laws governing them. Examples of these offices would be the consumer protection division of the city or county attorney's office. In Arizona, for instance, a specific example would be the Tucson City Attorney's Consumer Protection Division. It has the legal power to get restitution for the consumer, an injunction against questionable practices, and fines against the establishment.

State consumer offices are set up differently from state to state. Some states have a separate consumer department while others have a consumer affairs office as part of the governor's or attorney general's office, or both.

In California, the complaint procedure is posted in each repair shop. In Michigan, a written complaint can be filed with the Bureau of Automotive Regulation. In Arizona, a complaint can be filed with the Arizona attorney general's office. The procedure for filing complaints varies from state to state. Check with your state office for information.

When you file a written complaint, always include copies of any written estimates, work orders, bills or invoices, warranties, guarantees, cancelled checks, credit card receipts, letters, time and dates of phone calls, the names of the persons you talked to (service manager, receptionist, mechanic, etc.) and the dates, names of eye witnesses, and any other documents or information connected with your complaint. If complaining in person, bring any old parts that were returned to you and other evidence such as tape recordings. Muster as much documentation as possible.

If you want the repair facility to receive more than a slap on the wrist for a proven infraction, you must engage the assistance of an agency that has legal power to act against it. BBB, AUTOCAP or action lines are fine for filing and resolving complaints, but they have no legal power to fine or get restitution or close down a shop. You must complain to an agency that has those specific powers.

The *Consumer's Resource Handbook* is a must for those wishing to file complaints or pursue action against a business. I highly recommend it. It's published by the United States Office of Consumer Affairs and lists city, county, state, and federal consumer agencies, their addresses and phone numbers, along with many other private consumer complaint organizations and sources of help. It would be an excellent book to take on that long vacation or business trip. You can obtain a free copy by writing to:

CONSUMER INFORMATION CENTER
Pueblo, Colorado 81009

AN EXPERT'S VIEW
ON EFFECTIVE COMPLAINING

Remember when you were a kid and groused to Mom and Dad about doing homework or chores. Most of the time your whimpering was ignored. But occasionally, if you caught your parents in a good mood, or if the method you used to complain was tactful, you got what you wanted.

Well there is also a proper way to register your auto repair complaints. I doubt if the person who comes back to the shop and says to the manager, "This %##@(∗ car is running worse now than when I brought it to this &∗∧%#! shop; fix the !(∗&&%! thing!" would be welcomed with open arms, no matter if the shop was at fault or not. The way you approach the shop can have a lot to do with whether you get satisfaction or not.

In 1972, ASC's John Goodman was appointed by then Governor Ronald Reagan to help start up the California Bureau of Automotive Repair (BAR), a state agency that regulates the auto repair industry in California and provides consumer protection.

After the BAR's first year, Goodman wrote a report we alluded to earlier that was based on the first 100,000 complaints the Bureau received. It singled out three main areas of consumer dissatisfaction with the repair industry.

Fraud. When the shop charges for work not actually performed or the customer is told that extra work or parts are needed when they aren't.

Incompetence. Being charged for parts and labor by a bungling technician who has improperly diagnosed the problem.

Misunderstanding. Finding that unauthorized work was done and/or receiving a large repair bill when a small one was anticipated.

Goodman emphasizes that misunderstandings can be avoided. "Insist on a written estimate and don't give your O.K. unless you fully understand what is to be done and what the cost will be. Always leave a phone number where you can be reached. By doing this you will avoid that most unpleasant 5 o'clock surprise. Good communication between you and the technician is the key to preventing misunderstandings."

COMPLAINTS DO BRING ACTION

Some states require licensing of auto repair facilities. Some have each shop post in a conspicuous place the procedure for filing a complaint. Others offer assistance through toll free or pay hot lines which are an effective means of dealing with dishonest shops and resolving consumer complaints.

California's BAR handles over one million telephone inquiries each year. From these calls some 60,000 written complaints are filed. About half of these command state action and are usually resolved or closed within 30 days. The two most frequent complaints BAR receives? Failure of the repair shop to give the customer a written estimate or unauthorized work being done. Complaints can help get rid of dishonest operators and in many cases provide leads for agencies investigating fraudulent repair practices.

Tom McClory, assistant attorney general and head of the consumer fraud section of the Arizona attorney general's office, says his office is deeply concerned about auto repair fraud and makes a serious effort to police the problem.

"One of the best enforcement methods is to use undercover cars," says McClory. "Arizona and other states have enforcement units that use this technique. An unmarked car is thoroughly checked out by an expert mechanic. Then it's driven into a questionable shop or service station. The transaction is often recorded and even videotaped. The targets of these investigations are selected based on the number and type of complaints received. Our enforcement efforts have returned tens of thousands of dollars to victims of auto repair con artists. But we need to receive your complaints. We can't urge you strongly enough to report any suspicious or fraudulent activity to the appropriate agency to help us in the enforcement effort."

Arizona's Attorney General, Bob Corbin, believes that undercover operations that result from customers complaining about a specific garage do a lot of good. "Whenever we run an automotive undercover operation," says Corbin, "the effects are dramatic."

"But there has to be an ongoing type of investigation," says Michigan's Fred Pirochta. "It can't be done once and not expect the problem to surface again." It's your complaints that will keep the limelight on dishonest operators, bathing them with the publicity they loathe, until like mushrooms exposed to too much sunlight, they will shrivel up and close their doors. Complaints are the hinges on which effective consumer protective action swings.

But in the long run the automotive service industry itself must be responsible for its own actions and help guard against fraudulent schemes and incompetent shops that tarnish their image. The Automotive Service Council of California has strived to maintain such watchdog action over its members for the past 47 years.

Founded in 1940 by a group of 11 automotive repair shop owners who chalked a code of ethics on a garage floor, the group has steadily grown to its present 1500 member garages. Recently merged with the Independent Automotive Service Association, ASC and IASA combine to form the Automotive Service Association (ASA), a 10,000 member group with representation in every state.

The California ASC still abides by its own rules and ethics. Prospective members are screened before being accepted to the group, and ASC does not admit to membership shops which have too many complaints logged with the Bureau of Automotive Repair. Complaints against member shops are taken up by the organization staff. Infractions are punished and any member that refuses to live up to the standards imposed by the group is expelled.

ASC executives report that there are very few complaints against member shops. Martin Dyer, director of the California BAR, agrees, noting that the BAR rarely hears about ASC members.

It might take an industry commitment through groups like the ASC and ASA to police and discipline its members to restore customer confidence and trust in the repair industry. But until that time, it's still caveat emptor.

13

Preventive Maintenance

Honest, competent, and dedicated mechanics—and there are plenty of them—face terrible abuse when they recommend adequate preventive maintenance. "That's the same as doing repairs that aren't needed" is the accusation from the wary and the suspicious. We wonder how they would feel about flying with an airline whose policy it was to send airplanes to the maintenance hangar for a check-up only when one of its engines stopped running.

Ball joints sold but not needed can become front page news as a fraudulent automotive repair case. Ball joints needed but not sold can be found in the obituary column, as it is well established that unsafe cars can cause accidents. The terrible shame of highway fatalities is tied closely to the question of misunderstandings about preventive maintenance.

—John Goodman
"Anatomy of a Complaint"

Taking your car in for preventive maintenance is like going to a doctor for a checkup: there might not be anything major wrong with you at the time but small problems can be identified early when damage is minimal, and the price of the repair is low. The same with auto repair. You avoid the big one by having a series of less costly regular checkups and servicings.

There should be no misconceptions about preventive maintenance: a well-maintained car is safer and is an owner's first-line defense against rip-offs and unnecessary repairs or unneeded parts.

In the long run, a well-maintained car causes less trouble and costs less to operate. Regular maintenance minimizes repairs; it keeps your car out of repair shops, and if you don't have to take the car in so often, you lessen the chances of getting ripped off. Keeping the car out of the shop—except for maintenance—should be every car owner's goal.

"Every new car warranty carries a clause that specific maintenance services must be followed: otherwise the warranty is void. The vast majority of car owners follow the instructions religiously. Then, a remarkable thing happens," says Goodman. "As soon as the car is out of warranty, the entire concept of preventive maintenance stops. Thereafter, cars are fixed whenever they need to be fixed. . . . The remarkable part of this is that we are all so dependent upon our cars and yet we will risk having them stop running completely before we will give them the attention they desperately need."

How true and how unfortunate. It's funny how some car owners react to investing a little money and care in their vehicles. They don't mind spending $15,000 on new iron but balk at regular interval $20 oil and filter changes or spending $75 to have the car tuned. They become penny wise and pound foolish. Sure they save a couple of bucks by putting off the servicing. But these temporary savings are illusory for the neglect will come back to haunt them. Eventually, they pay the piper, either with expensive and unnecessary repairs, a lower resale value—or both.

Full service gasoline stations are getting hard to find. Where once you could fill up while the attendant checked the oil, battery, coolant, tires, wipers, and washed the windows, now self-service stations, with their emphasis on fast-in and fast-out, are proliferating. You pump the gas and you check the oil. Trouble is that most people are in too much of a hurry or don't want to get their hands dirty so these items are neglected. The car's soul is sacrificed for convenience and a few cents per gallon savings.

Add to that the fact that the number of dealership service departments has dwindled (see Figs. 13-1 and 13-2), and it becomes obvious that many of the traditional service outlets that supplied routine maintenance in the past aren't there to help anymore. It's a wonder—and a tribute to the manufacturers—that cars run at all.

Do you remember the guy on the TV commercial who said "You can pay me now or pay me later." That, in one simple sentence is what preventive maintenance is all about: you pay a little now so you don't have to pay a lot later.

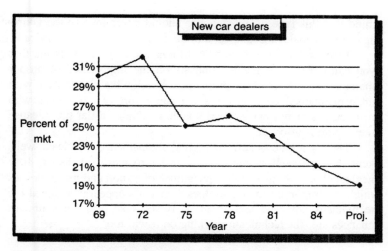

Fig. 13-1. Will the 15-year decline continue for new car dealers?

When a technician suggests that an item be replaced as a preventive step, he is not trying to sell you something you don't need. Within reason, it's better to replace something before it goes bad than to wait until it disables the car. A good example of this would be replacing fan belts and cooling system hoses at regular intervals. They might look good on the outside but if they have been on the car for a number of years, they should be replaced. However, keep in

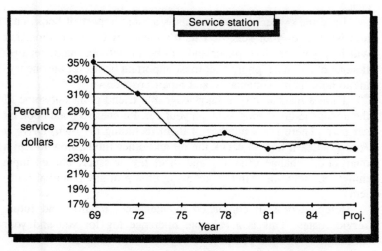

Fig. 13-2. Will service stations be able to hold their share as they have for 10 years?

mind that this type of maintenance should never involve the taking apart of any major mechanical unit on the car to inspect or service it.

Trooper Jerry Meyers of the Illinois State Police, tells me that you can't place too much emphasis on the importance of proper maintenance. "A lot of the problems we see on the highway are with undermaintained cars, and it's the same sort of car owner who neglects his or her car we find unable to change a flat tire because their spare is also flat."

There's a side benefit to regular maintenance. A clean, well-kept, and efficient-running car is easier to work on than a dirty neglected one. So just as the appearance of a shop and its employees might be important to you so does your car's appearance signal the technicians how you feel about it. If you take pride in your car, chances are, the technician working on it will too.

GETTING TO KNOW YOUR CAR

If you don't know a thing about your car and what makes it go, you place yourself in a very disadvantageous position. Turn the odds in your favor. Get to know your car and how it works. Learn what the major parts are and what function they perform. What will happen if one goes bad. Take a course in the basics of automobile upkeep. These are offered by community colleges; private consumer information groups; car clubs; city, county, and state consumer offices; new car dealerships; and trade schools. Many of them are no-cost or low-cost.

Read the owner's manual. This is a most important book, custom written for your specific car. It's loaded with information that will help your car last longer and run better without major repairs. It's one of the most ignored yet most important books for anyone trying to hold their maintenance and repair costs down.

Have a mechanic or a knowledgeable friend point out some of the under-the-hood geography on your car. Purchase a good book on car care. There are a number of them including my own, *Drive It Forever*. Learn how to check the oil and other fluids, how to add a quart of oil, change a flat tire, and check tire pressure. These simple things can help you avoid or keep you on top of any potential problems.

Keep records of completed maintenance, repairs, and future service dates. This is a valuable reference log for you and your mechanic—and for a prospective buyer of your vehicle.

REPAIRING THE HIGH-MILER—
DOING JUST WHAT IS "NECESSARY"

In "The Anatomy of a Complaint," John Goodman, singles out two areas that repair shop customers sometimes classify under the heading of "unnecessary repairs" but which in reality aren't. They are repair to the high-miler, and preventive maintenance.

Problems crop up when a customer brings a high-mileage car into a shop for repairs and wants just enough done to it to keep it going. That puts the mechanic in a tough spot.

When a new car won't start, or won't stop, or has a difficulty of any sort, it is usually easy to isolate and repair because all of the parts are new, writes Goodman. Once the culprit (bad part) is located, it is replaced with pretty good assurance that we have solved the problem.

When the same car has 80 thousand miles on it, it is an entirely different animal. Deciding what is necessary and what is unnecessary becomes a matter of infinite judgment. The customer's (plea), doesn't want to spend too much, just what is necessary is a common instruction. If he pays for a new set of plugs to replace the old ones that have 20 thousand miles on them and doesn't feel a surge of improvement in performance, he may feel that he was taken. Especially if two weeks later, his neighbor, who is a mechanic, replaces a 75 cent wire which makes all of the difference in the world. He is hard to convince that there was a need to have paid for any of the work done by the first mechanic . . . The truth, of course, is that there is an enormous judgment factor in repairing a high-mileage car. Do too little and the symptoms are still there. Do too much and the bill is more than the worth of the car. It is clear to us that misunderstandings over repair to the high-milers will cause a lot of anguish again this year.

The final decision to repair or not to repair rests with you. Study the pros and cons of the estimate and decide if it will be worth it, or would you be better off investing in a later or even new model.

Many high-mileage cars belong to people on limited incomes. They can't afford a newer model, their current car has to last, and they have no choice but to have it repaired. That's exactly where a lot of understanding and effective communication is needed between the customer and the shop.

14

Modern Cars and the Technician "Crisis"

"High-tech options such as antilock braking systems, traction control, and active suspension promise to improve customer satisfaction, but might also leave today's technicians ill-equipped to perform repairs unless steps are taken to update training methods" (Fig. 14-1).

That concern was expressed by a seven-member panel of industry executives speaking at a recent SAE show press conference.

Panelists stated that a complete rethinking of the service technician's training must be implemented immediately.

The person designing the present day and future car probably has a Ph.D. and is running computer-aided design/computer-aided manufacturing systems, said Charles Probst, Cybern Systems Co. president. The marketer of this car is most likely a MBA running a Lotus 1-2-3 spreadsheet program on his IBM personal computer.

The buyer of the car has maybe a bachelor's degree and an Apple computer at home. But the person we all expect to keep this car on the road on a daily basis probably does not have any degree at all. He or she has a set of tools and a voltmeter. If we're lucky, it's a digital voltmeter.

—"Technician's Dilemma,"
Automotive News, March 14, 1988

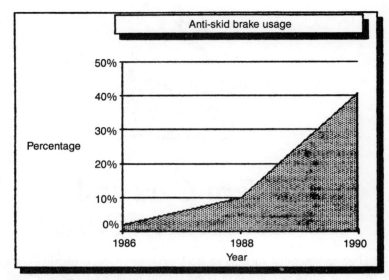

Fig. 14-1. Antilock brakes will increase to 40 percent of production.

Anyone vaguely familiar with the automotive aftermarket knows the auto service industry is facing a major problem: a lack of technicians qualified to work on today's and tomorrow's cars (Fig. 14-2). Scratch any automotive journal, and the blood of this shortage spurts out. And it's no secret to the average consumer that finding qualified auto repair technicians for the current crop of four-wheeled electronic marvels is no easy task. Just ask anyone who has had an engine-control module go out on them in a small country town.

Fig. 14-2. "Otto Mechanic" cartoon © 1988 BY JAY PIERSANTI. OLD CARS WEEKLY.

We are in the midst of an unprecedented automotive technological revolution. As mechanics wrestle with the new technology and its emphasis on electronics and computer controls, they also wrestle with our cars. New cars have become a training ground and experimentation lab for many technicians. Frequently, car owners pay the price for these uneducated probings.

As new car systems continue to evolve at a rate faster than most mechanics care to think about, specialization is rapidly coming to the fore. Just as today's doctor finds it impossible to be knowledgeable in all fields of medicine, so too there is growing awareness among today's mechanics that eventually they too will be forced into niches. The days of the old time, jack-of-all-trades mechanic are numbered.

Any time the new replaces the old something has to give. Current mechanics, unwilling or unable to cope with new technology, will be the first to go. According to Ron Weiner, president of the National Institute for Automotive Service Excellence, we are looking for a new breed of cat. The old stereotype grease-monkey won't be the same guy running and interpreting diagnostic equipment or repairing the high-tech machinery of the future. It will be tough making a hi-technician out of a knuckle-buster. As my grandmother would have said: "You can't make a silk purse out of a sow's ear."

Clarence's dilemma is typical of many mechanics. Clarence, working in a service station in Virginia, looked at my car but was unable to find the problem. He changed the fuel filter, sprayed the carburetor with cleaner and only charged me $2 for a half-hour of his time. He was honest and even apologized for not being able to help. Admitting he was stumped, he blamed it on "computer-controlled cars."

"Intimidation by computer" is a common mechanic's malady (Fig. 14-3). Their inability to fathom electronic components confounds them to a point where even the simplest ailment—such as my loose spark plug wire—is assumed to be something more complicated. I believe this electronic intimidation is the font of much incompetence.

Clarence won't be one of the new breed Weiner refers to. He, and thousands like him, will find other positions in the repair business, percolating down into the vast aftermarket with their still-needed skills. Demand for the more traditional-working, repair and maintenance mechanics will rise. According to the research group Frost and Sullivan, the specialty shop trades will be one of the fastest growing segments of the automotive service market. Specialty shops dealing in muffler, brakes, transmission repair, fast lube, tune-up,

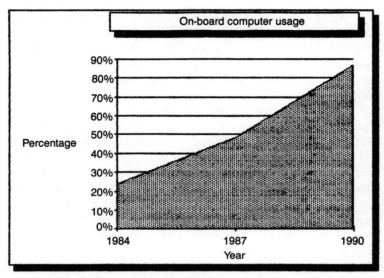

Fig. 14-3. Almost every car of the '90s will use an on-board computer.

tires, and shocks will continue to demand a supply of men like Clarence who can work with their hands.

Many mechanics don't have the desire to adapt to the new technology. Some are old, ready to retire in a few years, and will find ways to keep working on the older crop of more familiar cars. An older gentleman in WaKeeney, Kansas, told me after listening to my engine, "I'm a little dumb on these new cars with computers; I don't know what to look for, what to do. I'm glad I'm about ready to call it quits." Another service station attendant in Cranston, Rhode Island, slammed the hood in disgust after he couldn't find the problem. "These computer cars," he moaned, "got me going crazy."

Ron Weiner believes that the computer excuse is a cop-out of low-tech mechanics who are just hanging around. With a few days training a month, he believes they could keep up enough to be able to work on some of the newer cars. But many current mechanics complain that with the salary they are making and the demands that are put on them, it's just not worth it. "Why should I bust my buns for what they are paying me" grumbled a mechanic in North Carolina. "I'm not going to go out and pay for any training out of my pocket and come back here and earn the same amount of money."

"It's no secret there is a shortage of qualified service technicians industrywide," says Dick Hartzell, vice president of service, Nissan

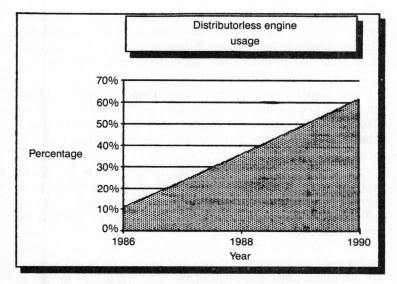

Percentage

70%
60%
50%
40%
30%
20%
10%
0%

1986   1988   1990
Year

Fig. 14-4. Distributorless ignition will increase to 60 percent of production.

Motor Corp., U.S.A. That growing need for high-tech mechanics was impressed on me time and time again. (Fig. 14-4). A person who can run and interpret basic diagnostic equipment is treated like royalty. "You'll have to wait until our scope or computer man gets here," was an all too familiar refrain. The high-tech boys are already held in esteem and hold a position separate from other mechanics.

The Automotive Information Council (AIC) estimates there are about 850,000 repair technicians currently available to service some 130 million cars on the road, a ratio of about one mechanic to 150 cars. John Scowcroft, director of technical affairs for the Motor Vehicle Manufacturers Association (MVMA), puts the figures somewhat higher at 1 million mechanics and 160 million cars, a ratio of one mechanic per 160 cars.

These cars and mechanics come together in about 115,000 service stations, 150,000 auto repair shops and some 25,000 new car and truck dealership service departments. Aftermarket service dealers (repair shops) account for a staggering 75 billion dollars annually in repair and service work.

U.S. Bureau of Labor statistics indicate that between now and 1995 the need for qualified technicians will rise faster than average. Around 40 percent (or somewhere between 300,000 and 400,000) more technicians will be needed, all highly trained, all specialists in high-tech auto repairs. Another industry spokesman estimates the current need to be even more dramatic, putting the figure at 600,000. These numbers are breathtaking. Where this army of highly trained electronically-adept technicians will come from is a question that makes industry experts cringe.

ASE's Weiner sees the technician shortage as a major problem but not one of crisis proportions. He believes the shortage will eventually be filled by technicians coming out of the trade and vocational schools, the community colleges, and in-house training programs instituted by the manufacturers.

What has seriously cramped the manpower supply, Weiner believes, is that during the past few years the nonautomotive high-tech industry has drained off prospective auto technicians. "We have lost a lot of people to computer servicing and other electronic-based service industries."

ASE, which has around 200,000 certified mechanics in positions around the country, currently has training programs in some 114 vocational schools throughout the U.S. and had prototypes in Florida and Ohio that dispense rigorous technical training with an eye to the future. In addition there are many independent schools and training services like Autotech (the "Graduate School" for auto technicians) and AMTS (Auto Mechanic Training Seminars) that are available to interested technicians. General Motors has training facility agreements with some 150 community colleges and vocational schools while other manufacturers have similar or in-house arrangements.

Repair industry trade organizations chip in by keeping their members on the leading edge of technological improvements. "With emphasis on training and retraining for automotive technicians," says Allen Richey, president of ASA, the nation's largest repair industry trade organization, "the Association strives to keep the industry competitive in the computer age. Education is now a matter of survival and is the major goal of the Automotive Service Association."

Why haven't more people responded to the call for high-tech, high-quality technicians? As Weiner points out, many have been grabbed up by the more glamorous and higher paying electronic service industries. Today's rank-and-file mechanic makes somewhere between 14 and 24 thousand dollars, hardly the pot at the end of the rainbow. But skilled, big-city technicians, properly equipped, can command from the high 20s to the mid 30s, while a superior diagnostic technician can double that. The ring, it seems, is there for

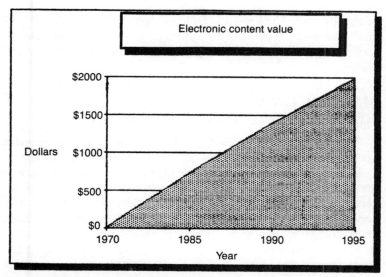

Fig. 14-5. By 1995, consumers will be paying for electronics in their cars—which will be reflected in their auto repair bills.

those who are determined enough and have the heads and hands to grab it.

Bob Dylan sang, "The times, they are a changin'." Well, the cars are a changin' right along with the times. Never before has the mechanic's ability to absorb new technology been more challenged. Years ago when a new engine or transmission was introduced it didn't take long before the know-how and parts to repair it filtered down into the aftermarket. Today, with changes coming with machine gun rapidity, the gap between the aftermarket and the manufacturer is wider than ever. James G. Vorhes, retired vice-president of General Motors customer sales and services, in a speech to the Congress of Automotive Repair and Service (CARS), noted that "There is a technological gap between our products and the aftermarket's ability to service them, and it's getting wider." Vohres estimates that by 1990 cars will have 5 times more computing power than 1987 models. A recent General Motors ad underscores that, trumpeting the fact that future GM automobiles will have electronic-instrument controls that project information onto a display nearer to the driver's line of sight, on-board self-contained navigational devices, electronic steering systems, computer-controlled suspensions, and electronic antilock brake and traction control units (Fig. 14-5). Because I test drive new cars daily, I know first-hand that much of that technology is already here. The Frost and Sullivan report, "The New Automotive Aftermarket," projects the electronic parts repair and replacement aftermarket to show the biggest increase of future aftermarket trades.

MANUFACTURERS ARE RESPONDING TO THE CHALLENGE

The widening gap between the new technology and the aftermarket's ability to service it is having ramifications in another area. Dealerships, traditionally ready and able to service customers' cars, are finding themselves ever more pressed with increasing loads of service work. In one dealership I visited in Southern California, the service writer politely chuckled when I asked him if there was any chance of getting my car in. "I have 17 cars ahead of you now and there's only an hour until closing. I already have another 25 lined up for tomorrow. I hope that answers your question."

COMPUTERIZED HELP FOR COMPUTERIZED CARS

Ford Motor Company's Service Bay Diagnostic System (SBDS) is an example of how manufacturers are responding to the call for high-tech rapid diagnosis and repair of automobile problems at individual dealership service departments throughout the country. When this system is in place at Ford and Lincoln-Mercury dealerships, it will enable a vehicle to "tell" the service computer what is wrong with it, and "instruct" the service technician how to fix it. Ford anticipates that all dealership service departments for the complete Ford lineup will have a direct computer link-up with SBDS by the early 1990s.

The SBDS will be hooked up to the vehicle's on-board computers to use direct vehicle computer information as a basis for diagnosis. It will then locate the source of the problem, and serve up the appropriate graphics and repair procedures. During this procedure, the SBDS will continuously survey an in-dealership database of service bulletins, shop manual procedures, vehicle history, vehicle graphics, and other pertinent information to provide the technician with the data needed. This database will be updated regularly through a Ford system in Dearborn, Michigan. SBDS will also contain a portable computer to assist the technician in identifying problems that are apparent only when the vehicle is being driven. SBDS, like the Allen Computer Engine Analyzers mentioned in chapter 4, will also be expert-system based.

Currently Ford technicians make use of the On-Line Automotive Service Information System (OASIS). Established in 1985, this computer-based service information system is the precursor to the SBDS. According to Emil A. Pulik, manager of Ford Parts and Service Division's Advanced Service Engineering Department, "The OASIS database contains everything that Ford knows about the servicing of our vehicles starting in 1981, all sorted by symptom and the specific attributes for each individual vehicle identification number."

To use the OASIS system, a service technician enters the vehicle symptoms and identification number into a data terminal with a keyboard and printer in the dealership that is connected by phone to the OASIS computer. OASIS then provides him with the latest repair information specific to the vehicle and symptom in question.

"In effect," says Pullick, "OASIS makes every service technician as smart as the smartest service technician. By recalling similar symptoms on similar vehicles and providing a list of probable causes and relevant service information, it speeds up and improves service operations. Repairs are done faster, and done right the first time."

OASIS currently receives an average of more than 10,000 calls a day from Ford and Lincoln-Mercury technicians.

FOR INDEPENDENTS, HELP IS JUST A PHONE CALL AWAY

Where does all this manufacturer high-technology leave the independents? Out in the cold? Not by a long shot, for new car manufacturers are well aware that they can't service each and every car they make, and they rely heavily on independents to do the vast majority of nonwarranty service and repair work (Fig. 14-6). It's to the manufacturer's advantage to share service information with independent shops, and service bulletins appear at dealerships and independent shops almost simultaneously.

In addition, some immediate relief for independent auto service shops has recently become available in the form of troubleshooting hot lines similar to the Ford OASIS program. The July 1988 AIC *Newsfocus* reports:

More and more automotive technicians discover these days that help is just a phone call away.

Mechanics who seek troubleshooting advice by calling tele-

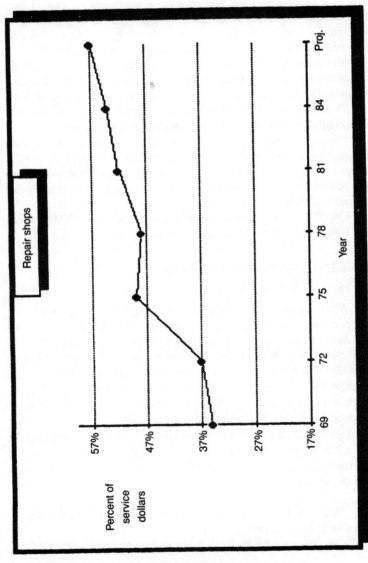

Fig. 14-6. Will repair shops continue to grow as they have for 15 years?

phone hot lines are a sign of the times, says Michael Duebner, technical services coordinator for the Automotive Engine Rebuilders Association. Cars are just getting more complex, and it is hard to keep up with an increasing number of specifications.

I think the frequency that these numbers are being used has increased industrywide, Duebner says.

AERA is one of the organizations experiencing an explosion in help calls—more than 300 a month this year (1988) compared with about half that in 1986.

The Automotive Parts Rebuilders Association, Automatic Transmission Rebuilders Association and several parts and equipment manufacturers are among others who have hot lines, Duebner says.

Such services relieve technicians of having to digest and remember too much information, says Dave Schuit vice president of the Midwest Technical Training Center, Chicago.

He says the long-term success or failure of these programs depends upon the future of the automotive aftermarket and the direction that the aftermarket takes.

These hotline technical services promise to be one solution to the aftermarket's dilemma (Fig. 14-7).

Tech-net

A diagnostic support service that provides:

- Factory service bulletins tied to problems
- Diagnostic support with a large computer database to improve diagnostic accuracy.
- Diagnostic experts that give technicians step by step guidance and continuous training, relating instructions to specific vehicle problems.
- Improves quality and profits while meeting the training demands of the new cars.

Fig. 14-7. Telephone hotlines provide high-tech help for independents.

THE PLYMOUTH/AAA
TROUBLE SHOOTING CONTEST

"Young people have lost interest in careers in automotive technology, and that's reflected in the shortage of auto mechanics. If the current trend continues, we may have a shortage of a million mechanics by the turn of the century," says John Moore, manager for the Plymouth/AAA Trouble Shooting Contest.

For years, AAA and Plymouth have awarded scholarships to encourage young people to enter careers in automotive technology. Since 1949, the Trouble Shooting Contest has placed more than 40,000 contestants in full- or part-time jobs as auto service technicians. The contest encourages students to develop the high caliber of expertise needed to repair today's complex, computer-controlled automobiles.

"The days of simple auto repair are over," says Moore. "Today, auto mechanics must have the ability to understand the functions of computers and the intricacies of engine performance."

According to the Bureau of Labor Statistics, an estimated 80,000 new automotive technicians are needed each year. "We have more and more cars on the road today, and fewer people going into automotive technology," Moore says. "So despite the increased need, we actually have about the same number of mechanics as we did 10 years ago."

Moore illustrates the problem with a story about a Washington, D.C. car dealership owner who went to Detroit to recruit top-notch automotive technicians. After two visits and extensive newspaper advertising, he returned to Washington with only two new employees.

"The industry is facing a quality, as well as a quantity, problem," according to Moore. "That's why the Trouble Shooting Contest is so important—it motivates youth to be interested in automotive repair, and also promotes quality in training."

The Trouble Shooting Contest encourages high school students to further their auto service training and to pursue careers as auto service technicians. Although it is obvious that all future technicians can't come from the Trouble Shooting pool, it is a step in the right direction. There is no question that we need qualified service technicians, and efforts like this pay off in getting those people into the trade where they are desperately needed.

As we have noted, dealers and large independent shops are getting more than their share of work on newer cars because of the tech-

The University of Michigan Transportation Research Institute projects the do-it-yourself market will decline. The responses of a delphi study panel were: Do-it-yourself market through 1995.

Likely trend	% of panel responding
• Overall decrease	43%
• Increase in minor maintenance Decrease in major repairs	32%
• Almost all DIY will be eliminated	21%

96% of the panel feels the market will be greatly reduced!

Fig. 14-8. Do-it-yourselfers won't be able to do it themselves anymore.

nician shortage and the aftermarkets' inability to catch up and service the new cars. And by introducing more sophisticated vehicles, major manufacturers are burdening their own service departments to overflowing, and whether by choice or happenstance, are culling out many small and large independents with outdated equipment and do-it-yourselfers (Fig. 14-8).

Do-it-yourselfers, the car owners who have always done their own repairs and service, are coming face-to-face with the new electronic technology. Many don't like what they see. What was once the province of the backyard, shadetree mechanic is now the domain of dealerships and large independent well-equipped garages. The do-it-yourselfer is being forced to take his or her car to places with the equipment and technical expertise to repair and service them. Besides changing the oil, waxing the car, rotating tires, and doing minor cosmetics, the do-it-yourselfer can do little to promulgate his love affair with his modern machine.

Additional burdens on the aftermarket are coming from the rapid change-over of full-service gasoline stations to self-service pumps with convenience stores attached.

I stopped at a large repair facility in Jacksonville, Florida that advertised engine repair and tune-ups. When I asked to have the engine checked out the owner said they no longer do engine work and were in the process of converting to a specialty shop dealing in shocks, tires, brakes, and alignments.

"Why no more engine work?" I inquired.

"The cars are getting too complicated, and it costs too much money to buy equipment to service and diagnose them," he said. "We can't find good men to keep up with the equipment and cars, and there are too many returns by customers not satisfied with the work done. To be truthful, we were losing money doing it."

But the electronic computer-controlled car, that marvel begat by government mandates for clean air and better fuel economy, has taken on an identify of its own. Bumper-to-bumper computer- and electronic-control and monitoring of all mechanical, hydraulic, and electrical components is the rule and not the exception. The new-wave car is here to stay—if only we can find the (new wave) technicians to keep them running.

Index

Allen's Smart Engine Analyzer
(SEA), 29-31
communicating symptoms to
mechanic, 33-36
diagnostics-only shops, 36
engine analyzers, 27-31
expert systems, 29-31
on-line automotive service information system (OASIS), 113
second opinions, 9, 35-36
service bay diagnostic system
(SBDS), 112
shop equipped for, 23
Smart Scope, 29-31
Tech-Net for, 115
Dietrick, Ron, 54
distributorless ignition, 109
do-it-yourselfers, high-tech cars and,
117
Drive It Forever, 2, 102
Duebner, Michael, 115
Dyer, Martin, 98

E

electrical system, shop equipped for,
22
electronics (see also high-tech cars),
xiv, 111
growth of, 21
locating service for, 18
shop equipped for, 22
emissions control system, rip-off
repairs to, 73
engine analyzers, 27-31
accuracy of, 28
accuracy of, multiple problems, 31
answers and more questions from,
29
competence of mechanic using, 28
expert systems and, 29-31
on-line automotive service information system (OASIS), 113
engine analyzers, scan tools, 27
service bay diagnostic system
(SBDS), 112
Tech-Net for, 115
engine control module (ECM) (see
engine analyzers)
engine repair, major, shop equipped
for, 23
engine repair, minor, shop equipped
for, 22
equipment, well-equipped shop, 20-23
Erf's Garage, 8
estimates, 9, 49-54, 82, 95
authorization of, 51

blank, 71
checking car out before paying, 53
example of, 50
final invoice from, 52
vague or incomplete, 71
ethics, 37-39
customer's, 39
repair shop, 37-39
Evans, David A., 11
expert systems, 29

F

Fair Credit Reporting Act, 60
fanbelts, 101
Federal Trade Commission
billing complaints and, 59
service contracts, 62-64
Ford on-line automotive service
information system (OASIS), 113
Ford service bay diagnostic system
(SBDS), 112
fraud and dishonesty, xii, 97
Reader's Digest 1986 survey, 1-10
registering complaints of, 9-10
safeguards against, 8-10
tricks to watch for, 65-80
fuel, 9
fuel injecton, 9
full service gas stations
15-year decline in, 101
high-tech cars and, 117
preventive maintenance and, 100
Furness, Betty, 1

G

General Motors customer sales and
services, 111
general repairs, shop equipped for, 22
Goodman, John, 68, 79, 96, 99, 100,
103
Griffith Shell, 8
guarantees, 49-53, 95
preventive maintenance and, 100

H

Hartzell, Dick, 108
Harvey, Paul, 1
heating/ac, shop equipped for, 23
help lines, 95
high-mileage vehicles, preventive
maintenance and necessary
repairs, 103
high-tech cars, 105-118
anti-lock brakes, 106
distributorless ignition, 109
do-it-yourselfers and, 117